YORK NOTES

Persuasion

Jane Austen

Notes by Dr Julian Cowley

 Longman

YORK PRESS
322 Old Brompton Road, London SW5 9JH

Pearson Education Limited
Edinburgh Gate, Harlow,
Essex CM20 2JE, United Kingdom
Associated companies, branches and representatives throughout the world

First published 1999
Tenth impression 2007

ISBN-13: 978-0-582-41463-1

Designed by Vicki Pacey, Trojan Horse, London
Phototypeset by Gem Graphics, Trenance, Mawgan Porth, Cornwall
Colour reproduction and film output by Spectrum Colour
Produced by Pearson Education Asia Limited, Hong Kong

Contents

PART ONE

INTRODUCTION   How to Study a Novel   5
                Reading *Persuasion*   6

PART TWO

SUMMARIES & COMMENTARIES
                Note on the Text   8
                Synopsis   8
                Detailed Summaries   10

PART THREE

CRITICAL APPROACHES
                Characterisation   70
                  Sir Walter Elliot   70
                  Lady Russell   71
                  Elizabeth Elliot   72
                  Mary Elliot   72
                  Louisa and Henrietta Musgrove   73
                  Mrs Smith   73
                  Mr and Mrs Musgrove,
                    the Crofts, the Harvilles   74
                  William Walter Elliot   74
                  Frederick Wentworth   75
                  Anne Elliot   75
                Themes   76
                  Economy and Extravagance   76
                  Risk and Caution   77
                  Selfishness and Mutuality   77
                  Pride   78
                  Personal Bias and Point of View   79
                  Situation   80
                  Constancy   80

Narrative Technique and Style
    Narrative Voice   **81**
    Satire   **81**
    Ambivalence   **82**
    Free Indirect Style   **82**
    Parenthetical Remarks   **83**
    Irony   **83**
    Theatrical Elements   **84**

PART FOUR

TEXTUAL ANALYSIS
    Text 1   **86**
    Text 2   **91**
    Text 3   **96**

PART FIVE

BACKGROUND   Jane Austen   **102**
    Her Other Works   **104**
    Historical Background   **105**
    The War against Napoleon   **105**
    The Changing Nature of Society   **105**
    Literary Background   **106**

PART SIX

CRITICAL HISTORY AND BROADER PERSPECTIVES
    Critical Reception   **108**
    Contemporary Approaches   **109**
    Feminist   **109**
    Historicist   **110**
    Post-Colonial   **110**

Chronology   **111**
Literary Terms   **115**
Author of this Note   **116**

PART ONE

INTRODUCTION

HOW TO STUDY A NOVEL

Studying a novel on your own requires self-discipline and a carefully thought-out work plan in order to be effective.

- You will need to read the novel more than once. Start by reading it quickly for pleasure, then read it slowly and thoroughly.

- On your second reading make detailed notes on the plot, characters and themes of the novel. Further readings will generate new ideas and help you to memorise the details of the story.

- Some of the characters will develop as the plot unfolds. How do your responses towards them change during the course of the novel?

- Think about how the novel is narrated. From whose point of view are events described?

- A novel may or may not present events chronologically: the time-scheme may be a key to its structure and organisation.

- What part do the settings play in the novel?

- Are words, images or incidents repeated so as to give the work a pattern? Do such patterns help you to understand the novel's themes?

- Identify what styles of language are used in the novel.

- What is the effect of the novel's ending? Is the action completed and closed, or left incomplete and open?

- Does the novel present a moral and just world?

- Cite exact sources for all quotations, whether from the text itself or from critical commentaries. Wherever possible find your own examples from the novel to back up your opinions.

- Always express your ideas in your own words.

This York Note offers an introduction to *Persuasion* and cannot substitute for close reading of the text and the study of secondary sources.

Jane Austen's novels have enjoyed sustained popularity in recent years. This is partly attributable to their 'period feel', their deft evocation of a way of life that no longer exists. As documentation of a bygone England, Jane Austen's fiction has enjoyed notable popularity amongst makers of costume dramas for cinema and television.

Persuasion is set in the south-west of England in the years immediately following the Napoleonic wars. Gallant naval officers, enjoying prosperity during peacetime, figure prominently in the novel's cast of characters, and are regarded with unequivocal approval.

Rather less admiration is extended to Sir Walter Elliot, a foolish minor aristocrat, whose financial problems provide the initial momentum for the plot. Sir Walter is the main focus for *Persuasion*'s **satirical** strand, but the main thread of the novel is a love story.

The romance involves Anne Elliot, now twenty-seven, and Frederick Wentworth, risen to the rank of captain during the recent conflict. Their earlier engagement was terminated following an act of persuasion by Lady Russell, a friend of Anne's late mother. Eight years having elapsed, fortune now throws the former lovers together again, and the novel traces an unfolding of events that confirms their reawakened passion.

The key question that confronts us is: 'Did Anne Elliot act correctly when she succumbed to Lady Russell's persuasion, and terminated her engagement to Frederick Wentworth?' In the late twentieth century, it is likely that we will regard the older woman's intervention as undue interference, and that we will feel inclined to assert the rights of the nineteen-year-old Anne to marry the man she loves. Of course, a different set of manners governed behaviour for a young woman of Anne's class at the start of the nineteenth century.

In the broader view, the question is whether Anne was correct to be governed by well-intentioned caution, or whether she would have been better advised to take a risk and follow the dictates of her heart. Should we follow the advice of our elders, or should we be ruled by our passions? Is there a middle course between these options, and if so how do we discover it?

We may prefer to place trust in instinct, but a crucial incident in the novel, Louisa Musgrove's accident on the Cobb in Lyme Regis, shows the harm that can follow from excessive impetuousity. We may discern the value of accepting guidance offered in a spirit of protective care. But if Anne Elliot was saved from financial insecurity when she rejected Frederick Wentworth, she was condemned to an agonising period of regret.

At the time that Jane Austen wrote this novel, there had been a marked shift in popular taste, away from **Augustan** values of restraint and rational decorum, towards **Romanticism** with its commitment to personal freedom and its focus upon intense feelings. Jane Austen's earlier novels had consistently affirmed an Augustan taste, but in *Persuasion*, her last completed work, she seems to have conceded some validity to the Romantic view. She steers such a careful course between those positions however, that ultimately it is left to us, as readers, to consider the case of Anne Elliot and Frederick Wentworth, and to determine whether we find ourselves for or against persuasion.

PART TWO

SUMMARIES & COMMENTARIES

Jane Austen began writing *Persuasion* on 8 August 1815. The first version was completed on 18 July 1816. The final, revised version was published posthumously, together with her satire of sentimental romance, *Northanger Abbey*, in 1818.

Modern editions are based on the standard text prepared by R.W. Chapman, and published in 1926. The Penguin Classics edition conforms to the consecutive numbering of chapters, from 1 to 24, which is now usual. The initial printing, in 1818, comprised two volumes, with twelve chapters in each. This format is preserved in the current World's Classics edition, published by Oxford University Press.

An alternative chapter, which survives in manuscript form, originally occupied the place now taken by Chapters 22 and 23. Both the Penguin Classics and the Oxford World's Classics edition additionally include the original ending, enabling comparison with that which eventually Jane Austen considered more suitable.

The text used in compiling these Notes is the Penguin Classics edition (1985).

SYNOPSIS

Sir Walter Elliot, of Kellynch-hall, is a widower with three daughters. Elizabeth, the eldest, and Anne live with him, while Mary, the youngest, is married to Charles Musgrove, and lives at nearby Uppercross.

Eight years previously, Anne became engaged to a naval officer, Frederick Wentworth, but was persuaded not to marry him by Lady Russell, a friend of her late mother, on the grounds that his prospects for advancement were limited. Financial constraints now force Sir Walter to let Kellynch-hall to Admiral Croft, whose wife is Wentworth's sister.

Sir Walter and Elizabeth take rooms in Bath, while Anne stays with Lady Russell at Kellynch-lodge, and with Mary at Uppercross

Cottage. At Uppercross, Anne finds herself regularly in the company of Charles Musgrove's parents, and his sisters, Henrietta and Louisa. Captain Wentworth visits his sister at Kellynch. He is invited to Uppercross by the Musgroves, who regard him as an attractive guest, and he shows interest in both sisters. He treats Anne with apparent indifference. Her distress at this is intensified when Henrietta restores her favours to her cousin, Charles Hayter, leaving the lively Louisa as the sole focus for Wentworth's attentions.

A party from Uppercross journeys to Lyme Regis, in Dorset, to visit Wentworth's friend, Captain Harville. Anne develops a friendship with Captain Benwick, who had been engaged to Harville's recently deceased sister, Fanny. Louisa Musgrove is severely injured in a fall. Anne remains calm, establishing order amidst the general panic. The party returns home, leaving Louisa in Lyme to convalesce.

Soon afterwards, Anne travels to Bath with Lady Russell. She finds that her father and sister have renewed acquaintance with their estranged cousin, William Elliot, who is heir to the Kellynch estate. On introduction, William and Anne recognise one another from a chance encounter in Lyme, where he had shown evident admiration for her. Sir Walter and Elizabeth direct their energies to cultivating the society of their distant relative Lady Dalrymple, and her daughter, Miss Carteret.

Anne, meanwhile, befriends anew her schoolfriend, Mrs Smith, now widowed, in ill health, and living in straitened circumstances. Anne is also preoccupied with the danger posed by the predatory Mrs Clay, who appears to have designs on her father. It is assumed by Lady Russell that William Elliot intends to propose marriage to Anne.

A letter from Mary conveys the startling news that Benwick has become engaged to Louisa Musgrove. Then, Captain Wentworth appears at Bath. His coldness towards Anne is clearly thawing, but the situation is complicated by William Elliot's attentions to her.

There are further arrivals in Bath: Mary and her husband, Mrs Musgrove, Henrietta, and Captain Harville. After conversing with Harville on the topic of constancy in love, Anne receives a letter in which Wentworth expresses his devotion to her. She is flustered, but agrees to marry him. Following the wedding, Wentworth and Lady Russell are reconciled. Mrs Clay goes to live in London with William

Elliot. Mrs Smith remains a close friend, her fortunes greatly improved by Wentworth's intervention. Anne and her husband enjoy great happiness in their married life.

CHAPTER 1   **Introduction to Sir Walter Elliot, his daughters, his neighbour Lady Russell, and his heir William Walter Elliot. Disclosure of Sir Walter's financial difficulties**

We are introduced initially to Sir Walter Elliot, of Kellynch-hall, in Somersetshire. His character is built upon his twin obsessions: social rank, and physical beauty. His own status and good looks are everything to him. As the narrator tersely sums him up: 'Vanity was the beginning and the end of Sir Walter Elliot's character; vanity of person and of situation' (p. 36).

We learn that he is a widower, aged fifty-four, and that he has three daughters: Elizabeth, Anne, and Mary. Mary is married to Charles Musgrove, and lives in the nearby village of Uppercross. The other sisters are unmarried, and remain at home.

Following Lady Elliot's death, the instruction of her teenage daughters fell largely to her close friend, Lady Russell. It was popularly supposed that this widow would marry the widower, but after thirteen years she and Sir Walter remain neighbours, and close friends.

The narrator shifts attention briefly to Anne Elliot, describing her early prettiness, and its subsequent fading. Her consequent loss of power to marry well has further diminished her father's low estimation of her. The focus moves to Elizabeth, upon whom Sir Walter's hopes for a prestigious marriage still firmly rest. At twenty-nine, she is two years older than Anne, but has retained her good looks. Elizabeth has been, in effect, the mistress of Kellynch-hall for thirteen years, and while devoted to her father, she is evidently eager to find a suitable husband.

We are told that the family's acquaintance with William Walter Elliot did not occur until he was a student of law. It is apparent that he holds his relatives in low regard, and avoids contact with them. Elizabeth envisaged that she would marry him, but the heir surprised his family by marrying a wealthy woman, said to be socially inferior. All communication with Mr Elliot ceased, but it is known that his wife has recently died. It is clear that Elizabeth would like to marry him, and so become Lady Elliot. However, her wounded pride, and his continuing contempt make the match seem unlikely.

An increasingly pressing fact of the family's life is that Sir Walter has serious financial problems. His extravagance is commensurate with his vanity, and the exercise of economy appears to him unnatural. Lady Russell and Mr Shepherd, Sir Walter's lawyer, are called upon to furnish advice.

Jane Austen establishes a comic tone: Sir Walter is a figure to be laughed at. But those qualities of conceitedness and snobbery which make him amusing, are clearly offered for our disapproval. This is the characteristic mix found in Jane Austen's social satire: detached amusement and engaged mockery.

Economy is a marked feature of this novel's style; Jane Austen says a great deal with minimal means. Here the reference to the 'Baronetage' enables her to outline the situation of the Elliot family with remarkable conciseness. Sir Walter's handwritten additions compound our sense of his fastidious character, but they also inform us of Mary's marriage to Charles Musgrove, and that the heir to his estate is William Walter Elliot. The laws of inheritance in Jane Austen's day did not make allowance for property to pass to female descendents. The Elliot sisters are not eligible for the estate. So, it is a socially significant detail that Kellynch will pass to their cousin. It is clear why marriage is such an important issue in *Persuasion*.

The satisfaction her father derives from the 'Baronetage' is counterpointed against Elizabeth's distaste for it. This passing observation is, in fact, a telling index of her uneasiness at remaining unmarried, especially as her cousin, the heir, has proved such a disappointing individual.

Jane Austen had achieved great skill in economical commentary by this stage of her writing career. She uses subtle nuance one minute, blatant criticism the next, in a bold yet highly effective manner. So the fastidious additions are followed by the declaration:

He considered the blessing of beauty as inferior only to the blessing of a baronetcy; and the Sir Walter Elliot, who united these gifts, was the constant object of his warmest respect and devotion. (p. 36)

Such combinations are successful largely because of the author's control of irony throughout the novel.

Her direct criticisms confirm the understanding we have picked up from more subtle clues carefully placed for us. Arguably, one of the pleasures of reading Jane Austen's fiction derives from such confirmation that we are reading correctly. She makes us recognise our own perspicacity in comprehending character and situation, while the characters themselves may be oblivious, or merely suspicious that all is not what it seems. Jane Austen is a great ironist, as well as a major **satirist**.

The narrator wryly observes that one genuine benefit derived from Sir Walter's handsomeness was that it helped secure a wife of superior character to his own. The heroine of *Persuasion* is to be Sir Walter's middle daughter, Anne, and if we are to have sympathy for her it is necessary that we do not associate her with the foibles of her father. We must perceive her as inheritor of the excellent qualities of her mother, whose only real lapse was her decision to marry a foolish man.

Jane Austen's characterisation is not merely a matter of portraying individuals in isolation. Characters are revealed through the relationships they hold with others. An alignment between certain figures can sound alarm bells as we read, and make us cautious in our judgements. Or it may confirm our impressions and enable us to discriminate appropriately.

So, our sympathy for Lady Russell is held in suspension: she was friendly with the evidently worthy Lady Elliot, but has remained friendly with the conceited Sir Walter. It is in her favour that she has not married him; it will be still more so if her closeness has been motivated primarily by the sense that she is a surrogate mother for his daughters. But it is soon apparent that Lady Russell shares some of Sir Walter's snobbish attitudes.

Crucially, Jane Austen manipulates characterisation in order to reflect upon Anne Elliot. The other characters' shortcomings and blind spots serve to throw into the foreground Anne's strengths of character. If Jane Austen had simply drawn her as a remarkably resourceful, sensitive, and intelligent woman, she would have run the risk of making her seem excessively idealised, and artificial. By constructing her in relation to the weaknesses of others, Jane Austen ensures that Anne becomes a firm, and credible moral centre for the novel (see Characterisation). Although Anne is by no means perfect, the virtues she embodies form a yardstick against which Jane Austen's satire does its work.

It is telling, then, that Sir Walter dotes upon Elizabeth, his eldest daughter, who most resembles him, while he views the others as inferior. Despite her 'elegance of mind and sweetness of character' (p. 37), Anne carries no weight with her father, '– she was only Anne' (p. 37). As well as furthering characterisation, such observations serve the novel's thematic concern with the ways in which a character's obsessions or prejudices result in blinkered or distorted perception of other people.

Sir Walter's money problems introduce a thematic concern with the benefits of moderation (see Theme on Economy and Extravagance). In the broader view, they also suggest a historical situation in which the influence of the minor aristocracy was giving way to the ascendancy of the professional classes (see Historical Background on The Changing Nature of Society). The need to find a solution for his problems initiates the sequence of events that forms the storyline of *Persuasion*.

the Baronetage probably Debrett's *Baronetage of England*, published in 1808

Dugdale Sir William Dugdale's *The Ancient Usage in bearing of such Ensigns of Honour as are commonly call'd Arms, with a Catalogue of the present Nobility of England ... Scotland ... and Ireland*, published in 1682

Tattersal's Richard Tattersal (d. 1795), who ran horse auctions, founded this centre for gambling on races in Grosvenor Crescent, in London. The building was demolished in 1866

CHAPTER 2   **A decision is made that Sir Walter should let Kellynch-hall and, with Elizabeth, take up temporary residence in Bath**

Lady Russell contrives, and Anne concurs, to persuade Sir Walter that the economies she proposes are in keeping with his dignity, and are of a kind suitable to members of his rank in society. But the stubborn baronet refuses to amend his style of living. When he says that he would sooner quit Kellynch-hall, the shrewdly opportunistic Mr Shepherd seizes the occasion, and suggests that such a departure would provide a satisfactory solution. Eventually, a temporary move is agreed upon.

Anne favours staying in the vicinity, in a more modest house. The decision, however, is to go to Bath. Lady Russell, who spends part of every winter there, rejects Anne's resistance to Bath. Lady Russell considers a move desirable also because she disapproves of Mrs Clay, Mr Shepherd's daughter, who has recently returned to the area, and has established a degree of friendship with Elizabeth. She distrusts this woman's skill in 'the art of pleasing' (p. 46).

> In her characterisation of Mr Shepherd, who is not to play a major role in the novel, Jane Austen seizes the chance to **satirise** the legal profession. His refusal to commit himself to definite advice may be taken as cautious pragmatism, but there are distinct hints that it is actually self-serving opportunism. Additionally, Shepherd's caution shows that he knows Sir Walter to be utterly self-centred and easily offended. As noted previously, Jane Austen's characterisation reverberates through a portrayal of relationships amongst a set of characters, rather than an outline of them in isolation (see Characterisation).

> So, Mr Shepherd's preference for deferring to Lady Russell's good sense in the formulation of a plan, supports the conventional view of her sagacity. But characterisation of Lady Russell also takes more direct form. She is discussed as a generally sensible, prudent, benevolent, and conservative person. We learn of her tendency to deliberate, rather than leap to quick decisions. This will assume greater relevance as we learn more of her role in Anne Elliot's personal history. Like Shepherd, Lady Russell is alert to Sir Walter's snobbish sensitivity and pride. There is a

suggestion that she understands him so well because, to a lesser degree, she shares the baronet's dedication to rank and its privileges. That also will prove to have been germane to her relationship with Anne.

Lady Russell is methodical in calculating the kinds of economy required, and unlike the others she consults with Anne, whose clear-sightedness and honesty are made evident in her reported response. It is evident that Lady Russell's recognition of Anne's worth is testimony to genuine good sense, although we may find reasons to distrust the commonly held evaluation of her wisdom.

The novel's thematic concern with benefits derived from moderation is indicated in Anne's preference for removal to a modest house nearby. Although Bath was a less fashionable resort than it had been fifty years earlier, Anne appears to associate it with unnecessary extravagance, and to recognise the potential expense it might incur (see Theme on Economy and Extravagance). Perhaps it is more pertinent that, in Chapter 4, we learn that Anne stayed briefly in Bath following the termination of her engagement to Wentworth, so the place has unhappy associations for her. It is typical of *Persuasion* that an apparently objective rationale for making a certain choice is bound up with a highly personal bias (see Theme on Personal Bias and Point of View).

Lady Russell favours Bath and overrides Anne's objections, which she considers groundless prejudice. It is **ironic** that in granting authority to her own taste, she denies the validity of Anne's taste. She appears benevolent in her ambitions for Anne to enter a wider social circle, presumably in order to meet a potential husband, but it is clear that such benevolence is more easily demonstrated because it accords with her own wishes.

The presence of Shepherd's daughter, Mrs Clay, who is certainly not to Lady Russell's taste, may be taken as a further example of the lawyer's efforts to manipulate the situation to his own advantage. The real reasons for Lady Russell's dislike of the woman are open to speculation. It may be that she is exercising her acknowledged skill in discriminating character. It may be that she is anxious to

CHAPTER 2 continued

ensure respect for Lady Elliot's memory by keeping an unworthy successor to that title at bay. It may be that she sees a need to guard the daughters from an unwelcome, intrusive influence. Or is it that she is jealous, conscious that her role as family adviser is compromised by Mrs Clay's proximity? There are other possibilities. Finding the right way to read Lady Russell's motivation is a major challenge posed to readers throughout *Persuasion*.

CHAPTER 3   **Mr Shepherd and his daughter, Mrs Clay, persuade Sir Walter that a naval officer would make a suitable tenant. Admiral Croft and his wife apply to rent Kellynch-hall, and are accepted**

John Shepherd points out that the end of the recent war should result in wealthy naval officers seeking temporary homes, and that should facilitate the letting of Kellynch-hall. Mrs Clay, who has accompanied her father, supports his view that naval officers make careful and respectful tenants. Sir Walter maintains his haughty attitude towards the very notion of having a tenant.

The first applicant is Admiral Croft, whom Shepherd met at the quarter sessions in Taunton. In the course of persuading Sir Walter, the lawyer delineates Croft's familial background, making him appear the ideal tenant for Kellynch-hall. Anne is able to add information concerning his naval career.

We learn that Croft's wife has a brother who once lived nearby, as curate of Monkford. Anne supplies the name of Mr Wentworth. Her father points out that in his view, Wentworth was not properly a gentleman, having neither property nor connections. Shepherd judiciously drops that line of persuasion. Sir Walter succumbs to others, and feels that an admiral is of sufficiently high standing to make a respectable tenant, without threatening his own superiority.

Anne is unsettled by the agreement. A flush comes to her cheeks and, as she walks in the garden, she anticipates the arrival in her own home of a certain individual: 'a few months more, and *he*, perhaps, may be walking here' (p. 54).

If the decline of the gentry forms a broad historical backdrop to the story, Jane Austen adds a more specific historical strand to her novel with reference to the recent Napoleonic wars (see Historical Background). National feeling at the time was strongly supportive of the British navy and its actions, so Jane Austen could assume that contemporary readers would regard the nautical characters in *Persuasion* as representatives of positive values.

Anne speaks up in support of the navy, in light of the service it has rendered to the common good, at some cost to its members. At the time of first publication, this would undoubtedly have convinced readers of Anne's personal worthiness, but as we are soon to learn, her view has profoundly personal relevance. The formation of point of view is again prominent amongst Jane Austen's concerns (see Theme on Personal Bias and Point of View).

Confirmation of this may be found in Sir Walter's position; while acknowledging the utility of the service he adds, 'I should be sorry to see any friend of mine belonging to it' (p. 49). This aloof snobbery has a palpable bearing upon Anne's situation, as we shall soon learn. The navy is objectionable to Sir Walter on two counts: it allows men of lowly birth to achieve eminence; and it ages them prematurely. These two points are, as we have already seen, his twin obsessions. Jane Austen could rely upon those readers who shared Anne's view to feel a sense of amused outrage at Sir Walter's facile dismissal of these defenders of the nation.

But the war was not just a matter of honour; it was also an arena in which considerable personal fortunes could be made by professional sailors. That fact is crucial to the story, as it enables Frederick Wentworth to advance his social standing. It is **ironic** that such advancement contributed further to the decline of the older landed families.

Shepherd's fortuitous meeting with Admiral Croft seems too great a coincidence, given our knowledge of his efforts to persuade Sir Walter of the desirability of just such a tenant. The Admiral is very rich, and Shepherd is keen to assist in his plans. Jane Austen leaves us in no doubt that the lawyer is self-serving in his concern to please others, but there is also a lurking suggestion, never explicitly made, that this professional man is actively manipulating the course of events for his own advancement.

Anne's evident knowledge of Croft's career, and of nautical matters more generally, is, as we are soon to discover, intimately related to her own recent history and subsequent concerns. Her knowledge of the name of the curate, Wentworth, is also significant. Events are conspiring to produce an **irony** of situation, which will confront her with her own past, embodied in the figure she anticipates anxiously as the chapter ends.

a rear admiral of the white the navy was divided into three squadrons (red, white, and blue). The white was second in seniority

Trafalgar this important naval battle was fought, off Spain, on 21 October 1805. It established British naval supremacy for the next hundred years

the East Indies islands in South-East Asia, which were a rich source of raw materials for European trade

the deputation legal authority to kill game on an estate

CHAPTER 4   **An account of Anne Elliot's love affair with Frederick Wentworth, and its abrupt termination. A summary view of Anne's feelings during the intervening years**

The narrator reveals that the 'he' in Anne's mind is Frederick Wentworth, a naval officer and brother of the curate formerly at Monkford. He had lived there also for six months in 1806, and became engaged to Anne. When the prospect of marriage was revealed to Sir Walter, for his consent, he met it with 'all the negative of great astonishment, great coldness, great silence'. He considered that his daughter, at nineteen, would be wasted on such a man. It would be 'a very degrading alliance' (p. 55). Wentworth had no social connections, and no wealth. His opportunities for advancement were confined to his profession, with all its uncertainties and risks.

Lady Russell concurred in deploring the alliance, and made a concerted effort to persuade her favourite amongst Lady Elliot's daughters to abandon the relationship. The engagement was broken, and Wentworth left the country. As a consequence, Anne suffered a loss of her good looks. The current action takes place some eight years later. Time has softened, but by no means removed, the painfulness of the experience.

Anne's memory of Frederick Wentworth had overshadowed all subsequent encounters with eligible men. Charles Musgrove had asked her to marry him, and was rebuffed, before being accepted by her sister, Mary. At twenty-seven, Anne feels she was wrong to have been swayed by persuasion when nineteen, although she refrains from apportioning blame.

From the navy lists and newspapers, Anne has learnt that Wentworth has prospered, has been promoted to captain, and has made a sizeable fortune. She is greatly agitated by the news that Mrs Croft, who is Captain Wentworth's sister, will soon be resident in Kellynch-hall. She takes comfort from the perception that neither her father and sister, nor Lady Russell seems conscious of the connection between current developments and this crucial event in her life.

Jane Austen uses the voice of the narrator to give a retrospective account of a traumatic event in Anne's life. A number of clues, which have been laid during the first three chapters, now take definite shape as we learn of her engagement to Wentworth, and of the pressure put upon her to end the relationship. The narration grants us insight into Anne's inner state, the continued turbulence of her emotions, and the efforts of her mind to come to terms with the direction events have taken. In such passages Jane Austen employs **free indirect style**, in ways that anticipate the sophisticated techniques for rendering psychological states used by later novelists such as Henry James and Virginia Woolf (see Narrative Technique and Style on Free Indirect Style).

The most enduringly affecting aspect of the novel is that in a social circle dominated by extraordinary selfishness, Anne sustains deep feelings of attachment for another person. Jane Austen poignantly observes that Anne 'had been forced into prudence in her youth, she learned romance as she grew older – the natural sequel of an unnatural beginning' (p. 58). At the time Jane Austen wrote this novel, fashionable literary taste had endorsed **Romanticism**, which often explored inner turmoil, and extreme emotions. *Persuasion*

CHAPTER 4 continued

caters to that taste, to some extent, although the author's more seasoned interest in how emotions are held in check by manners and rational judgement is equally present.

As her devotion to Wentworth becomes increasingly evident during the course of the novel, the obsessions which motivate those around her seem increasingly deplorable. At this stage, we are made aware of her constancy, which assumes the air of authenticity, while the insensitivity to her feelings shown by her father, sister, and Lady Russell marks them as her moral inferiors. Note that Lady Russell favoured a marriage between Anne and Charles Musgrove. This would have brought Anne more closely under her influence, while removing her from that of Sir Walter and Elizabeth, for whom, it becomes clear, Lady Russell has less respect than is commonly accepted.

the action off St Domingo the British had won a naval victory here in February 1806

CHAPTER 5   **Arrangements are made for the Crofts to commence residence at Kellynch-hall. Sir Walter and Elizabeth depart for Bath, accompanied by Mrs Clay. Anne stays in Uppercross with her sister, Mary, and visits the Musgrove family**

Arrangements are made for the letting of Kellynch-hall, to the mutual satisfaction of both parties. The Elliots begin to make plans for removal to Bath. It is agreed that Anne will divide her time between Lady Russell and Mary until the time comes to accompany Lady Russell to Bath.

Lady Russell is alarmed at the arrangement for Mrs Clay to accompany Sir Walter and Elizabeth. Both she and Anne fear that Sir Walter might be lured into marriage with the lawyer's daughter. Anne warns her elder sister of such a danger, but is ignored.

Anne stays with Mary in the old-fashioned village of Uppercross. Despite Mary's claim that she is not well, the sisters walk to the Great House to visit Charles Musgrove's family.

Jane Austen makes comedy from the highly conditional praise

expressed between Sir Walter and Admiral Croft. The sailor is characterised as bluff, worldly, and kindly. The contrast makes our sense of the baronet's pomposity more acute.

Elizabeth's terse remark, 'Then I am sure Anne had better stay, for nobody will want her in Bath' (p. 61) tells us a good deal about Elizabeth's own character, but Jane Austen has prepared us to read her comment **ironically**, so it should not diminish our sense of Anne's real worth. In fact, such disparagement of Anne only persuades us to regard her more highly, while the detractors are characterised as self-centred and blinkered (see Characterisation).

Mary, also is recurrently dismissive of her sister in a way that seems determinedly stylised on the author's part, rather than an attempt at naturalistic characterisation. Similarly, when Anne tells Mary that she had to visit the villagers before her departure, as they desired it, her own characterisation seems to be idealised, or sentimentalised, to the point of **caricature**. Is the author enjoying a joke at Anne Elliot's expense, at such moments? Certainly there are times when she appears almost unfeasibly good, in a world of folly and silliness. At other times, minor flaws in her character are indicated, in order to make her more credible. After all, a perfect heroine would not require our sympathy, and Jane Austen wants us to share something of Anne's emotional upheaval.

Anne acts as the voice of caution in advocating that Elizabeth be wary of Mrs Clay, whose intentions she distrusts. There is comic effect in the complacency with which the elder sister replies that there can be no real danger of an unwelcome engagement because Sir Walter has commented adversely on Mrs Clay's freckles. But as well as confirming, in the long term, Anne's superior powers of discrimination, the exchange highlights her real moral superiority to Elizabeth: 'There is hardly any personal defect,' replied Anne, 'which an agreeable manner might not gradually reconcile one to' (p. 63). With characteristic common sense, Anne concludes that drawing her sister's attention to the danger could do no harm in the long term.

She is similarly commonsensical in dealing with Mary's illness, which is magnified out of all proportion by her share of 'the Elliot self-importance' (p. 64). Her husband, who is used to her behaviour, has gone out shooting. She has dismissed her two small boys, for whom she has little time, even when she is well. It becomes apparent in their conversation that Mary is an attention-seeking hypochondriac, but Anne, with her usual resourcefulness, makes a measured and ameliorative response.

The Musgrove family is shown to embody a transitional phase in English identity: the parents live in an older style, the offspring have assumed the new. We are told that Anne feels no envy of the freedom and access to pleasures of the teenage Musgrove girls, but it is clear that their friendship as sisters is a matter of envy to her. Despite the assertion that she is not envious, we should not forget that Anne Elliot has developed in her maturity a taste for romance that was denied her in her youth. The Musgroves demonstrate an easy hospitality that is in clear contrast to her own family's painful self-awareness.

CHAPTER 6   **Overview of Anne's experiences with the Musgroves. The Crofts take up residence, and there is news that Frederick Wentworth is soon to visit his sister, Mrs Croft**

Anne adapts to the rather different way of living she encounters amongst the Musgroves, and finds herself acting as confidante to most members of that family.

At the end of September, Kellynch-hall is occupied by the Crofts, and Anne is preoccupied with Frederick Wentworth's possible presence in the vicinity. The Elliot sisters are invited to visit the Crofts and are welcomed hospitably. Anne learns that Edward Wentworth, the curate, is married, and she is flustered to hear that one of Mrs Croft's brothers is expected at Kellynch soon. Louisa Musgrove confirms that it is Captain Wentworth.

We learn that the late Richard Musgrove, an evidently troublesome brother of Charles, Henrietta and Louisa, had served under Frederick Wentworth. Anne is thrown into inner turmoil by the Musgroves' avowed determination to invite the Captain to join them, as soon as possible, to demonstrate their gratitude for the kindness he showed towards their wayward son.

The chapter opens with Anne's observations concerning how a change of company leads to a change in conversation. Amongst the Musgroves, she becomes acutely aware of the triviality of matters of concern at Kellynch-hall. The Musgroves have their blind spots and their vanities, but they are notably less concerned with rank than the Elliots, and they are a popular local family.

Anne perceives the importance of 'knowing our own nothingness beyond our own circle' (p. 69). This is clearly a perception that contrasts sharply to the self-importance of her father, in his parochial seat. In a novel that is extensively concerned with personal obsessions, this affirmation of critical detachment is striking. The factors which shape point of view, and which have such strong influence upon our sense of who we are, lose their shaping power if we move to another context, or enter another frame of values. Anne feels that it is proper 'that every little social commonwealth should dictate its own matters of discourse' (p. 69) (see Theme on Situation).

Another relevant issue raised here is the extremely limited sphere of Anne's experience. She has been confined within a domestic world, in a rural location. Part of the attraction for her of the lives led by sailors is undoubtedly the allure of distant lands, and the comparative vastness of the horizons of their experience. In Chapter 23, Anne will make explicit her consciousness of leading an almost cloistered existence, the fate of many women of her class. It is surely a consequence of this limited experience that she places such value upon 'the extraordinary blessing of having one such truly sympathising friend as Lady Russell' (p. 69). Without dismissing Lady Russell's value as a friend, Jane Austen certainly builds a picture of her which undermines an uncomplicated sense that she is a 'truly sympathising friend'.

The narrator suggests that Charles Musgrove has qualities to admire, but that these are often subordinated to his devotion to

CHAPTER 6 continued

sport. This state of affairs is attributed to his unfortunate marriage, the implication being that if he had been successful in courting Anne he would have developed into a wholly admirable individual, whereas the marriage to Mary has diminished him. This extends Jane Austen's strategy of making Anne the co-ordinating centre for positive values in the novel.

Certainly, the fact that she is taken so readily to become confidante for all members of the Musgrove household consolidates the sense that she is self-evidently reliable, trustworthy and honest. Mary, by way of contrast, is portrayed as a singularly unsuitable mother.

The service of Richard Musgrove on a vessel commanded by Wentworth is a clear contrivance of **irony** of situation. It provides an additional reason for the Captain to become a visitor to the Great House, and to be a topic of conversation in the social circle Anne has entered. Richard's lack of suitable qualities to become a successful seaman enhance, through contrast, our sense of Wentworth's character.

none of your Queen-squares for us an ironic reference for the benefit of the author's intimates, as the Austen family stayed in this square in 1799

CHAPTER 7   **The Musgrove family sings the praises of Frederick Wentworth. Mary's eldest son is hurt in a fall, and Anne organises the nursing care, while anxiously anticipating an encounter with Wentworth. He is evidently looking for a wife, but seems to have accepted that Anne has shown herself unsuitable**

Mr Musgrove meets Captain Wentworth at Kellynch, and admires him. Mutual dining arrangements have been made. Anne is agitated at the prospect of an imminent encounter. An early encounter is avoided due to an accident, in which her eldest nephew dislocates his collarbone and hurts his back. Anne is pleased to be kept busy attending to the child.

Henrietta and Louisa Musgrove sing the praises of Wentworth, who has won their affections. On the next day, Charles and Mary dine at Mr Musgrove's house, in the company of Frederick Wentworth. They return, brimming with enthusiasm for their new acquaintance.

Wentworth is to join Charles for breakfast at the Great House, after which they will go shooting. It seems that Wentworth has declined to join them at their cottage, on account of possible inconvenience following the child's injury. Nonetheless, he pays a courtesy call early the next morning, and Anne feels relief that the ordeal of meeting again is so soon over.

The narrator grants us insight into Wentworth's feelings that Anne had wronged him: 'She had given him up to oblige others. It had been the effect of over-persuasion. It had been weakness and timidity' (p. 86).

Anne's domestic usefulness, so evident here, and so emphatically contrasted to her sister's lack of maternal ability, barely conceals the amorous passion that has been aroused by Wentworth's proximity. She is occupied with speculation as to his feelings. The options she considers – indifference to her, or unwillingness to renew their acquaintance – betray, through **ironic** inversion, her hope that he will desire a reunion as keenly as she does, despite her ostensible reluctance. A mixture of dread and longing characterises her attitude.

Wentworth's initial reluctance to call at Uppercross Cottage, may show his considerateness with regard to the sick child. But his subsequent appearance suggests that curiosity concerning Anne has at length overcome reticence. Certainly, Anne's response indicates the perpetuation of old emotions: 'Alas! with all her reasonings, she found, that to retentive feelings eight years may be little more than nothing' (p. 85).

Mary reports Captain Wentworth's response to a question concerning Anne, that he found her 'so altered he should not have known you again' (p. 85). Her sense that he is not changed, unless for the better, results in 'silent, deep mortification' (p. 85). Jane Austen is again making telling comparison the core of characterisation, but shrewd readers may detect hints that beneath the contrast lies intense agitation shared by Anne and Wentworth.

Wentworth feels that Anne no longer has any power over him. He wishes to marry and settle down, and is available to any suitable young woman, with the exception of Anne Elliot. But she is evidently present in his thoughts when he specifies to his sister, Sophia Croft, that he is looking for 'A strong mind, with sweetness of manner' (p. 87). In establishing the distance between the former lovers, Jane Austen is preparing the ground for a resurgence of the passion which both are initially keen to refute. Her key technique of **irony** is essential to this process; we have come to recognise by this point that we should look for meanings other than the obvious.

CHAPTER 8   **Anne and Wentworth are regularly in the same company. The seafaring life is discussed. Anne plays the piano while the others dance**

Anne Elliot and Captain Wentworth find themselves 'repeatedly in the same circle' (p. 88). References in the conversation, particularly to the year of their engagement, inevitably bring their former relationship to Anne's mind and, she imagines, to his.

The Musgrove girls make inquiries about Wentworth's life at sea. His response necessarily highlights details that raise acute memories for Anne. The former lovers do not converse beyond civilities, despite the fact that eight years before, 'there could have been no two hearts so open, no tastes so similar, no feelings so in unison, no countenances so beloved'. Their new relationship seems to Anne to be 'a perpetual estrangement' (p. 88).

In conversation with Admiral Croft, Wentworth expresses his determination that women would not be allowed on board vessels under his command; his reasoning is that an appropriate level of comfort could not be assured. Mrs Croft enters the argument, accusing him of folly, but he will not be swayed. Mrs Croft affirms the pleasures and happiness of her life at sea with her husband.

Anne, as usual, plays the piano so others may dance. Her eyes fill with tears, but she is glad to be allowed to go unobserved. Henrietta and Louisa Musgrove, and their Hayter cousins, are all smitten by the dashing captain. Anne is aware that Wentworth has made casual enquiries about her, but generally she is tormented by 'His cold politeness, his ceremonious grace' (p. 96).

Jane Austen's strategy of significant contrasts works with particular effectiveness in distinguishing the current relationship between

Anne and Wentworth from that which existed eight years previously. The couple's feelings toward one another and their attitudes to those around them are to form the dramatic focus of the book.

In the course of Wentworth's conversation with the Musgroves the subject of marriage tellingly recurs; it is evidently central to his concerns. Is this because his recently acquired wealth and status persuade him of the need for domestic stability? Or is it possible that the renewed encounter with Anne has made him peculiarly sensitive to the marital state, which he so nearly entered eight years previously?

When the discussion turns to the lamentable Richard Musgrove, Wentworth responds in a sympathetic fashion, which only Anne recognises as a deliberated act of kindness. Her affinity with Wentworth is apparent, as well as her general perceptiveness. Mrs Musgrove, in particular, is too close to her son's memory to discern the truth of his worth. Once again, perception is shown to be inextricably related to point of view, and point of view to be shaped by often irrational biases (see Theme on Personal Bias and Point of View).

Wentworth argues against the presence of women on board ship. He considers that their personal comfort would be compromised beyond what is acceptable. His gallantry appears to be offered for admiration, but his sister sounds a far more practical note: 'But I hate to hear you talking so, like a fine gentleman, and as if women were all fine ladies, instead of rational creatures' (p. 94). It is possible to detect a feminist voice in Jane Austen's fiction at this point (see Contemporary Approaches), but it is equally the voice of practical experience, highlighting the idealistic nature of Wentworth's views. The fact that he is not married becomes significant. If he were, his adherence to the dictates of a code of conduct might be subordinated to the kind of pragmatic relationship which has sustained the happiness and contentment of Admiral Croft and his wife over a number of years.

Jane Austen, adopting a comic tone, makes fun of the narrowness of vision found amongst those who, unlike naval personnel, have not travelled far and extended their horizons. In fact, her own experience of the world was extremely limited. In Chapter 23, Anne makes impassioned comments upon the narrowness of opportunity available to women of her class.

Anne's readiness to play the piano is an instance of characteristic selflessness, so untypical of her family. But it can also be seen as an exhibition of her intense self-consciousness: she is eager to escape from possible contact with Wentworth. The narrator grants us access to 'some of the thoughts which occupied Anne, while her fingers were mechanically at work' (p. 96). A later novelist, such as Dorothy Richardson (1873–1957) or Virginia Woolf (1882–1941), might have presented directly the workings of the character's consciousness, but the literary conventions of Jane Austen's time were restrictive in that respect. Jane Austen's sustained commentary upon interior states, including her use of **free indirect style,** may be seen to be as an important step towards the subtleties of later **psychological realism.**

Note how the physical attractiveness of Captain Wentworth is made evident through the excitement he arouses amongst the young women of Uppercross, rather than through substantial direct description.

CHAPTER 9   **Charles Hayter sees Captain Wentworth as a rival for the affections of Henrietta Musgrove. Anne, looking after the children, finds herself alone with Wentworth. Hayter arrives, increasing the general uneasiness. The Musgrove sisters arrive, and Anne departs, highly unsettled**

Wentworth stays longer than he intended at Kellynch, the local hospitality apparently inducing him to delay proceeding to visit his brother Edward, in Shropshire. Charles Hayter, a cousin of the younger Musgroves, arrives at Uppercross, and is disturbed by the universal adulation for Wentworth, especially as he now appears to be a rival for the affections of Henrietta.

Hayter arrives buoyant with the news that the rector of Uppercross has agreed to engage him as his curate. This appointment should have smoothed the path to his marriage, but, with Wentworth present, Henrietta displays only marginal interest in him.

Anne has to endure a discussion between Mary and Charles Musgrove as to which of his sisters is likely to win Frederick Wentworth in marriage. Mary snobbishly disparages Charles Hayter, and consequently favours Henrietta for Wentworth.

One morning, at Uppercross Cottage, Wentworth finds himself unexpectedly alone with Anne. After an awkward exchange, Hayter arrives, adding to the uncomfortable situation. Mary's youngest child, Walter, appears, and hinders Anne, who is attending to his invalid brother. Wentworth, without comment, intervenes to free her from the infant's grasp. The Musgrove sisters enter the room where their ostensible suitors await them, and Anne takes the opportunity to leave, deeply flustered.

> Wentworth's decision to stay longer than intended at Kellynch-hall appears not to have been influenced by his renewed acquaintance with Anne, but in retrospect we may view his decision as a significant point in the gradual reawakening of his latent passion for her.
>
> The introduction of Charles Hayter is important, because his current situation has parallels with that of Wentworth eight years earlier. Hayter desires to marry Henrietta Musgrove, but as a poor curate with uncertain prospects he cannot be sure of her acceptance, nor of her family's approval. The Hayters are very much the social inferiors of the Musgroves. In contrast to Sir Walter's attitudes, the Musgroves allow no snobbery to prejudice their view of their daughter's suitor, but his ability to make material provision for her future *is* a pressing consideration.
>
> Anne exhibits sympathy for the young curate's situation: 'she had delicacy which must be pained by any lightness of conduct in a well-meaning young woman, and a heart to sympathize in any of the sufferings it occasioned' (p. 101). Her response may be a measure of her genuine altruism, or of the capacity for a particular kind of sympathy which her own experience of lost love has created. But we should not overlook the possibility that it may indicate a less noble, essentially jealous, concern that Henrietta

should not win Wentworth. Her subsequent agitation is a telling index of the intense feelings that still colour her perception of him.

Note that Mary's two-year-old son is called Walter. His stubborn misbehaviour acquires an added element of humour through that evocation of his grandpaternal namesake. It would seem that the deplorable qualities which Mary has so evidently inherited from her father have been further transmitted to his grandson.

CHAPTER 10 The Musgrove sisters, Mary and Anne, Charles Musgrove and Wentworth walk in the countryside. Anne observes the Captain's growing warmth towards Louisa. Wentworth learns from Louisa that her brother was refused by Anne before he married Mary Elliot. Returning home, he intervenes to secure a ride for Anne in Admiral Croft's carriage

Anne continues to observe and evaluate the relationship between Captain Wentworth and the Musgrove sisters. She does not discern his love for either, and adjudges their present attraction to him to be excited admiration rather than feeling which will endure. Charles Hayter chooses to withdraw temporarily, and Anne considers that wise.

One day in November, the sisters arrive at Uppercross Cottage, announcing they are going for a long walk. Mary and Anne decide to accompany them and, returning early from hunting, Charles Musgrove and Wentworth join the party. Anne is agitated once again, and tries to distract herself with recollection of poetry. Repeatedly, however, her attention is drawn to the lively conversation between Wentworth and the sisters. She notes a greater warmth towards Louisa.

Reaching the top of a hill, they have a view over Winthrop. Mary and Henrietta, who has become suddenly self-conscious, express a wish not to proceed further towards the home of Charles Hayter. But it is decided that Musgrove and his sisters should visit their aunt. The others remain on the hill.

Louisa soon returns and persuades Captain Wentworth to join her in collecting nuts from a hedgerow. Anne overhears a conversation between the young woman and Wentworth.

The group reassembles, with the addition of Charles Hayter, who has evidently experienced a reconciliation with Henrietta. There are now three couples, plus Anne. They encounter another contented couple – the Admiral and Mrs Croft, driving in their carriage. Following Wentworth's considerate intervention, Anne is offered a lift. Despite the Admiral's haphazard driving, the Crofts deliver Anne safely home.

Anne's efforts to make detached analysis of the burgeoning relationship between Wentworth and the Musgrove sisters are in part a means to exercise control over her still powerful feelings towards him. Anne is set up as something of an authority on matters of the heart, despite her limited experience. It seems that after the trauma of her broken engagement, she has devoted herself to efforts to reach a rational understanding of the rules which might govern love affairs.

More generally, Anne's detachment from romantic involvement throughout the previous eight years seems to have resulted in a tendency to make considered moral judgements. Often, we see her pondering a specific case, romantic or otherwise, and drawing a generalised conclusion from it. Her own life has been dramatically affected by Lady Russell's application of general rules for prudent conduct to her particular experience. Anne appears to have devoted much of her time to acquiring insight into the relationship between general rules and specific instances. This might appear to be a strength in her character, but remember that in Chapter 6, Anne recognised 'that every little social commonwealth should dictate its own matters of discourse' (p. 69). That insight would appear to limit the authority of generalised conclusions.

There is a distinct element of perversity in Mary's character. If an assumption is made concerning her, she will assume the opposite position. The Musgrove sisters' assumption that Mary would not wish to join them firmly commits her to going. Anne is unable to dissuade her, so, with evident foresight, she agrees to go with them in order to accompany Mary home once she has decided that she has walked far enough. Contrast continues to consolidate their characterisation (see Characterisation).

Despite his earlier comments with regard to precluding women from travel on his ships, Wentworth is particularly impressed by Louisa Musgrove's remark concerning his sister: 'If I loved a man, as she loves the Admiral, I would be always with him, nothing should ever separate us, and I would rather be overturned by him, than driven safely by anybody else' (p. 107). The devotion shown by Mrs Croft towards her husband is a centre of value in this novel. Louisa additionally wins Wentworth's approval by showing herself willing to take risks, for the sake of love. Inevitably, he will compare this reckless faith that love overcomes all with Anne Elliot's cautious retreat into security eight years previously.

Soon afterwards, Mary asserts to him that she has been to the Hayter's house only once or twice in her life, and she laments having such relatives. Wentworth clearly recognises the characteristic Elliot snobbery that compounded the effects of persuasion, and was in large part responsible for the severance of his relationship with Anne. His recollection of her is thrown into sharp contrast with the free-spirited vivacity of Louisa, who is evidently far less confined in her views than Anne Elliot was at nineteen.

Drawing contrast between the sisters, he says to Louisa: 'Your sister is an amiable creature; but *yours* is the character of decision and firmness, I see' (p. 110). It becomes increasingly clear as the novel develops that this remark is less an honest appraisal of the young woman than a veiled criticism of his treatment by Anne. He sees, for the moment, in Louisa, those qualities he hoped for and found lacking in the young Anne Elliot. This becomes explicit with the declaration: 'It is the worst evil of too yielding and indecisive a character, that no influence over it can be depended on' (p. 110).

Most telling of all is a thinly disguised reference to Anne's loss of youthful beauty, consequent upon her seeming fickleness: 'If Louisa Musgrove would be beautiful and happy in her November of life, she will cherish all her present powers of mind' (p. 110). The implied criticism is consolidated when Louisa comments adversely on the Elliot pride which Mary manifests. The Musgroves wish that Charles had married Anne instead. Wentworth is clearly intrigued by the fact that such a proposal was made, and that Anne refused. Louisa reveals that her parents were disappointed, and that they believe Lady Russell persuaded Anne to turn Charles down.

Wentworth intervenes to secure a lift for Anne, evidently perceiving that, as she is alone with three couples, she is bound to feel self-conscious and uncomfortable. Once in the carriage, she is aware that 'she owed it to his perception of her fatigue, and his resolution to give her rest'. She is suddenly convinced that although he cannot forgive her, he cannot be indifferent to her: 'it was an impulse of pure, though unacknowledged friendship' (p. 113). The Captain's act of considerateness is another indication that his surface coolness conceals an attraction to her, and concern for her that remains very strong. There is **irony** in the increasingly evident lack of congruence between what is said, and what is felt by the former lovers.

Irony of situation arises when Anne finds herself sharing a carriage with the couple whom Louisa has praised as ideal. This irony is heightened when the Admiral's conversation turns to a prospective marriage between Wentworth and one of the girls; but there is an indictment in his passing remark: 'And very nice young ladies they both are; I hardly know one from the other' (p. 114). His wife's muted praise suggests that she considers neither a really suitable match for her brother. Indications are made that Wentworth's apparent enthusiasm for Louisa is a provisional response to immediate and past circumstances, and that a basis for an enduring relationship has not been formed.

CHAPTER 11   **The party from Uppercross pays a visit to Wentworth's friends Captain and Mrs Harville, at Lyme Regis. Anne engages in friendly conversation with their friend Captain Benwick**

Lady Russell's return is imminent, and it is arranged that Anne should join her at Kellynch. Anne anticipates that she will see less of Wentworth there, as he spends so much time at Uppercross. Importantly, she wishes to avoid encounters between Lady Russell and the Captain.

Wentworth pays a brief visit to his good friend, Captain Harville, who has settled with his family at Lyme Regis, twenty miles away. On hearing this, even though it is November, the Musgrove sisters, their brother, Mary, and Anne accompany Wentworth to Lyme for an overnight visit. The narrator sings the praises of the seaside town and of its environs. Chief amongst the town's features is the Cobb, a stone jetty, which the party determines to investigate.

Wentworth introduces the Uppercross group to Harville, his wife, and their friend Captain Benwick, who served as first lieutenant on Wentworth's vessel, the *Laconia*. Benwick was engaged to Fanny Harville, his friend's sister, and is now in mourning for her. The Harvilles welcome all hospitably to their cramped lodgings. Anne is struck by the happiness of their home, even in these temporary surroundings.

During the evening, Anne talks at length with Benwick who displays a discriminating sense of literature that is much to her taste.

> The death of Fanny Harville is a sad case of situational **irony**. Throughout *Persuasion*, the risks taken during a naval career are emphasised; marriage to naval officers involves evident uncertainties. Yet Benwick not only survives, but has been promoted, while the woman to whom he was engaged did not live to witness his advancement. The cautious persuasion to which Anne succumbed is cast in an ironic light by the fate of this young couple: we might see a parallel in the fact that Wentworth too has been promoted while Anne's emotional life has effectively stopped. The dramatic suggestion to be drawn from the parallel is that Anne endures a kind of living death.

> But the parallel Anne herself recognises is between herself and Benwick; they have both endured loss of a loved one, an ironic correspondence, with the perceived difference that Benwick is 'younger in feeling, if not in fact' (p. 119). Her self-absorption at this point becomes still more apparent in the harrowing awareness that had she not rejected the admirable Wentworth, these estimable people would have been her friends also.

> At the Harvilles' home as at the Musgroves' she is struck by the warmth of hospitality, which reflects upon the absence of such welcoming goodwill in her own family.

> It has been noted before that Anne has a tendency to draw large conclusions from her consideration of specific cases. We might

detect in this tendency the influence of Lady Russell, who has served as a pontificating role model for her. In conversation with Benwick, assuming the guise of an authority on suffering, Anne hopes to be able to offer him helpful advice. There is genuine sympathy here, but also an attempt to transform her own suffering to a positive end for her own consolation.

We have seen in Chapter 10, how Anne found refuge in poetry when agitated by Wentworth's presence. Benwick shares her taste for literature and Anne suggests that 'it was the misfortune of poetry, to be seldom safely enjoyed by those who enjoyed it completely; and that the strong feelings which alone could estimate it truly, were the very feelings which ought to taste it but sparingly' (p. 122).

The poetry in question is evidently the product of **Romanticism**, fashionable at the time *Persuasion* was published, rather than the restrained **Augustan** verse of the late eighteenth century. The form of Anne's advice may show the influence of Lady Russell, but the message conveyed is indicative of Anne's desire for passion in her life. **Ironically**, that desire may be seen as another consequence of Lady Russell's influence, of the persuasion that ended Anne's engagement.

Jane Austen comments rather archly that Benwick is pleased by such recognition of his situation, as if suffering itself can afford a form of pleasure if it meets with sympathy. Anne suggests that the young captain should add prose to his diet of reading, and names a number of works that she considers will benefit him. There is a detachment in the narration here which verges on cruelty to the characters, and Anne is shown to be capable of priggishness which may momentarily qualify our sympathy towards her.

The concluding sentence is revealing:

When the evening was over, Anne could not but be amused at the idea of her coming to Lyme, to preach patience and resignation to a young man whom she had never seen before; nor could she help fearing, on more serious reflection, that, like many other great moralists and preachers, she had been eloquent on a point in which her own conduct would ill bear examination. (p. 122)

> **Marmion** or **The Lady of the Lake** poems by Sir Walter Scott (1771–1832).
> Marmion was published in 1808, Lady of the Lake in 1810
> the **Giaour** and **The Bride of Abydos** poems by Lord Byron (1788–1824). Both
> were published in 1813

CHAPTER 12   Anne and Henrietta walk by the sea. Wentworth and Louisa join them. Leaving the beach, Anne is conscious of being admired by a gentleman, and is aware that Wentworth has noticed the admiring look. It is discovered that the gentleman is William Walter Elliot. In the course of a final walk before departure for Uppercross, Louisa falls on the Cobb and is badly injured. Anne takes control of the situation. Arrangements are made for Louisa to stay with the Harvilles, attended by Charles and Mary. Wentworth accompanies Anne and Henrietta to Uppercross, where he breaks the news to Louisa's parents, before returning to Lyme

Next morning, Anne and Henrietta stroll by the sea and enjoy watching the tide coming in. Wentworth approaches, with Louisa. As they leave the beach, a gentleman looks at Anne with evident admiration. She is aware that the bracing air at Lyme has restored some of her former attractiveness. It is clear that Wentworth has noticed the stranger's admiring glance.

The gentleman is encountered again at the inn, where the party is staying. He is in mourning, but his interest in Anne is obvious once more. Completing breakfast, the members of the Uppercross group notice the stranger leaving Lyme in his carriage. Upon enquiry, they learn from a waiter that the gentleman is Mr Elliot, and they conclude it to have been William Walter Elliot, the heir to Kellynch-hall. Mary is especially excited by the coincidence.

After breakfast, the group, their number augmented by the Harvilles and Captain Benwick, take a final walk around Lyme before their scheduled departure for Uppercross. Anne and Benwick continue their discussion concerning the relative merits of Walter Scott and Lord Byron. Harville subsequently thanks her for drawing his friend out of his melancholy state. He tells how Wentworth broke the terrible news of Fanny Harville's death to Benwick, and stayed with him a week to ensure he survived his grief. Parting from the Harvilles, the group pays a last visit to the Cobb. Moving to the Lower Cobb to shelter from the wind, Louisa insists on jumping, to be caught by Wentworth. After doing so once, she repeats the action, in spite of his advocating caution. A miscalculation leads to her falling and injuring herself severely. She appears lifeless. Wentworth holds her; Mary is sure she is dead; Benwick and Anne support Henrietta as she faints.

Anne supplies smelling salts and practical advice, exhorting Benwick to help Wentworth. Charles Musgrove also tries to help. Anne is the steady centre once again. Benwick runs, on her suggestion, to fetch a surgeon. The Harvilles arrive, after seeing Benwick running in evident alarm, and they organise transportation of Louisa to their lodgings, where she is put to bed.

The surgeon confirms that she will survive, and the assembly grows calmer. The Harvilles offer to look after Louisa and to accommodate all others who wish to stay. Wentworth is now sufficiently composed to organise the group. He will take Henrietta home and break the news to her parents. Mary and Charles remain with Louisa.

Anne joins Wentworth and Henrietta in a chaise hired for their return journey. Wentworth conducts himself with studied calmness, only once allowing an outburst of remorse at his failure to prevent the accident.

They soon arrive in Uppercross. Anne is pleased that Wentworth asks for her approval of his plan – to keep Henrietta with her in the carriage, while he breaks the news to her parents, allowing time for their distress to settle. The Musgroves show admirable self-possession and, his mission accomplished, Wentworth heads back to Lyme and to Louisa.

As she strolls on the beach with Anne, Henrietta affirms the beneficial effect of being by the sea, and then turns her remarks to the specific case of Dr Shirley, the rector at Uppercross. With seeming altruism she comments that it might be a good idea for him to retire permanently to Lyme, which so admirably assisted his recovery from recent illness. The real reason for her elaboration of this scenario is in fact self-interest; she envisages an imminent future in which Charles Hayter will become rector of the village, and she will live comfortably as his wife. One of the book's persistent thematic concerns is the way in which seemingly selfless positions are assumed for basically selfish reasons, even by those characters for whom we feel sympathy (see Theme on Selfishness and Mutuality).

Henrietta says that while she fears Lady Russell's cleverness, she has great respect for her, and wishes Lady Russell were in a position to exert her famous influence over the old rector, persuading him to retire. The **irony** of this declaration can scarcely be lost on Anne, whose prospects for marriage, far from being improved, were blighted by her friend's persuasive skill. Henrietta's remark shows that Lady Russell's reputation is widely recognised; a less charitable view might regard this as a measure of the extent of her interference in local matters.

Wentworth notices the admiring glance that Anne receives from a passing gentleman. His response, although momentary, indicates that he is acutely conscious of Anne's presence, despite his ostensible preoccupation with Louisa. It is as if he regards the stranger as a rival for Anne's affections. As the novel progresses, this proves to be the case.

It is a bold stroke of situational irony that contrives the chance encounter at Lyme with William Elliot. Statistically improbable, such coincidence is a common feature of fiction, enabling the plot to be advanced speedily and in a concentrated way. It is still more common in stage plays, with their temporal limitations (see Narrative Technique and Style on Theatrical Elements). Anne calmly suggests that her father and his heir have not been on such terms as to make an introduction desirable. It is arguable that Jane Austen is depicting her heroine as altogether too habitually cautious; Anne might benefit from a little more impetuosity. She is secretly gratified that the heir to her father's estate has all the appearance of a gentleman, and a sensible one. She is also flattered to have been noticed, not least because of Wentworth's evident concern at this development.

Anne's conversation with Benwick concerns the relative merits of two eminent yet distinctive writers: Walter Scott and Lord Byron. It is not simply an engagement by Jane Austen with literary taste of the day; she is pursuing the process of comparative evaluation which is evident everywhere in *Persuasion*. In their literary discussion, the distinctive qualities of one author are discerned through contrast with the other.

Such comparison is, as we have seen, an important part of Jane Austen's characterisation in this novel: nobody is seen in total isolation; there is always a context for the judgements we form. We are told that Anne and Benwick, weighing the poets, are 'as unable as any other two readers, to think exactly alike of the merits of either' (p. 128). We might conclude from this that Jane Austen is aware that no two readers of *Persuasion* will come to exactly the same conclusion concerning its characters. There will be broad agreement but, as we have noticed, aspects of character are often not entirely what they seem to be, and there is room for variation in response.

Having said this, a consensus might be expected based on the characters' actions. Wentworth's scrupulous considerateness towards the bereaved Benwick shows real depth of loyalty and compassion. Actions of this kind are an essential part of the characterisation of Wentworth, just as they are of Anne, who looks after Mary's children, and tries to help her friend, Mrs Smith. Actions in *Persuasion* speak louder, and far less equivocally, than words.

Anne shows her worth in the relative composure she exhibits following Louisa Musgrove's fall. Previously in the book, we have seen Mary's eldest son injured in a fall. The correspondence of these incidents underlines the childishness of Louisa's actions. She lacks mature judgement, and suffers accordingly. The suggestion was made earlier that Anne might benefit from being more impetuous. That position seems to be contradicted by the consequence of Louisa's wilful refusal to succumb to persuasion.

A crowd gathers, and Jane Austen allows herself to indulge in a sardonic observation: 'many were collected near them, to be useful if wanted, at any rate, to enjoy the sight of a dead young lady, nay, two dead young ladies, for it proved twice as fine as the first report' (p. 131). This borders on bad taste, and seems to disclose a cynical view of human beings. Certainly, it makes genuine acts of compassion, and relationships of true mutuality seem especially valuable when they do occur. It also indicates that Louisa will survive – Jane Austen would surely not make so light of a fatality.

Recovering from the initial shock, Wentworth takes over from Anne as the figure in control of this situation. The resourcefulness, clear-sightedness, and good judgement they share is demonstrated through their behaviour. They appear superior characters, whose alliance is something we should endorse.

Their superior qualities are highlighted through contrast with Henrietta's feebleness and Mary's customary perversity. When it is proposed that Mary should return to her children, she is characteristically insistent on staying with her husband in Lyme. Anne is then persuaded to return to Uppercross, although she has had the satisfaction of hearing Wentworth argue that she should be asked to look after Louisa: 'no one so proper, so capable as Anne!' (p. 133). She is moved by the endorsement, partly because she is so taken for granted at home, but more because it confirms that the focus of Wentworth's attention is upon her.

Wentworth's decision to deliver the news to the Musgroves recalls his service to the Harvilles in telling Benwick of Fanny's death. He undoubtedly has the capacity to fulfil such a difficult task with delicacy and tact; that is a crucial aspect of his character. But we might expect that a man who cared passionately for Louisa Musgrove would wish to remain at her side. The reality of their relationship seems not to conform to common perception of it.

Anne, with that disarming detachment which we have come to recognise as one of her less appealing traits, wonders whether Wentworth would now modify his former view of 'the universal felicity and advantage of firmness of character; and whether it might not strike him, that, like all other qualities of the mind, it should have its proportions and limits'. Pointedly, she concludes her musings with the thought that 'it could scarcely escape him to feel, that a persuadable temper might sometimes be as much in favour of happiness, as a very resolute character' (p. 136). There is an element of self-justification here, of course. Anne seems to espouse the classic **Augustan** virtues of moderation and restraint, but underlying her judgement we may perceive real passion for her former lover, which accords more with the values of **Romanticism**.

an Emma towards her Henry in *Henry and Emma, a Poem, upon the Model of the Nut-Brown Maid* by Matthew Prior (1664–1721)

CHAPTER 13   **Anne joins Lady Russell at Kellynch-lodge. They visit Admiral and Mrs Croft at Kellynch-hall**

During her two remaining days at Uppercross, Anne makes herself useful to the Musgroves. Louisa's condition is reported to be stable and on course for steady recovery. Anne, before leaving, persuades the Musgrove family to go to Lyme in order to relieve their anxiety and to assist with Louisa's care. Left alone in the Great House, with November rain falling outside, she is plunged into melancholy reflection upon the fluctuating emotions she has witnessed at Uppercross.

She joins Lady Russell at Kellynch-lodge. Her friend notes the improvement in Anne's looks. The women discuss the accident at Lyme. Lady Russell determines to visit the Crofts at Kellynch-hall. Soon after arrival there, Lyme again becomes the topic of conversation. Anne learns that a note she received the previous day had been brought to Kellynch in person by Wentworth, and his sister tells Anne that he had made a special enquiry after her well-being.

Soon after this visit, the Crofts depart to visit friends in the north of the county. As they are unlikely to return before Anne accompanies Lady Russell to Bath, she feels safe from the painful prospect of seeing Wentworth in Kellynch-hall, or in uneasy company with Lady Russell.

Alone in the Great House at Uppercross, Anne muses on the prospect of its rooms following Louisa's full recovery:

> A few months hence, and the room now so deserted, occupied but by her silent,
> pensive self, might be filled again with all that was happy and gay, all that was
> glowing and bright in prosperous love, all that was most unlike Anne Elliot!
> (p. 138)

It is rare to see any character in this novel in physical isolation, but here Anne assumes the character of the solitary figure familiar in **Romantic** literature. That guise is accentuated by the November rain falling outside, in what might be seen as an example of what John Ruskin later called **pathetic fallacy**.

Anne's self-pitying mood suggests falsity in her customary calm demeanour. In Chapter 12, Anne felt that Louisa Musgrove should have acceded to persuasion and not taken an unnecessary risk. Here we see how Anne's allowing herself to be persuaded into caution has left a legacy of profound unhappiness. In Louisa's case, as in that of little Charles Musgrove, who also fell, it is clear that time will heal the damage done. It is equally clear that time has so far failed to ameliorate Anne's wounded emotions.

Lady Russell is apprehensive on account of Wentworth's recent presence in Anne's company, and it is with relief that she notes, and comments upon, the improvement in Anne's physical appearance.

It is **ironic** that this revitalisation of her looks, which her friend takes as a sign that she has not been unduly disturbed by Wentworth's return, is probably due to the revival of her passion for him.

Discussion of the events at Lyme necessitates mention of Wentworth's name. Anne finds it easier to talk of him after she has noted his apparent attachment to Louisa. The response to this news is remarkable:

> Lady Russell had only to listen composedly, and wish them happy; but internally
> her heart revelled in angry pleasure, in pleased contempt, that the man who at
> twenty-three had seemed to understand somewhat of the value of an Anne Elliot,
> should, eight years afterwards, be charmed by a Louisa Musgrove. (p. 140)

Lady Russell's nastiness at this point is striking. What sympathy can we feel, what respect can we retain for a woman with such a capacity for viciousness? Perhaps we should detect in her 'angry pleasure' an emotional registration of the discomfort she has felt since her intervention to terminate Anne's engagement. She has obviously witnessed the decline in Anne's spirits and attractiveness during that period, and must have been conscious of her responsibility for that suffering. We are seeing here not a rational reaction, but an emotionally charged thrill that her acts of persuasion were justified. Wentworth's involvement with Louisa has become Lady Russell's personal vindication.

The disparity between her surface composure and her interior state is consistent with similar duality in the characterisation of Anne and Wentworth, thinking characters who also have a capacity to feel deeply. The difference is, of course, that Lady Russell's submerged sentiments do not engage our sympathy.

The prospect of a visit to the Crofts at Kellynch-hall casts Lady Russell's renowned good sense still further into doubt. In her snobbishness, she envisages that the meeting will be a painful experience. Anne, who has formed an opinion of the Crofts so high that she feels they have a stronger claim to such a house than her own family, looks forward to the visit. Anne's low esteem for her father and sister is a critical response to their snobbery, the very quality which her friend now displays so blatantly. The basis for friendship between these two women is not always self-evident, and this will become a more jarring state of affairs when the harmonious and sympathetic relationship of Anne and Wentworth becomes more firmly established.

It is stressed that Anne thinks highly of Admiral Croft's 'goodness of heart and simplicity of character' (p. 142); Lady Russell, on the other hand, is not able to approve of his 'tone'. This not only rounds out the characterisation of the Admiral; it also refines our sense of the two women and the contrasting values to which they aspire. In making another telling contrast between characters, Jane Austen injects a typical element of **satirical** humour: the Admiral comments wryly upon the number of looking-glasses he has found in Sir Walter's room. These are now in storage.

It is significant that the note referred to in this chapter was delivered in person by Wentworth, who enquired especially after Anne's health. Ostensibly delivering news of Louisa to a woman whose interest he believes to be sincere, this is more profoundly a continuation of the contact with Anne which he values for its own sake. He has, after all, left Louisa behind in Lyme. That departure accrues greater significance as the novel progresses. Anne remains unsure how to interpret his actions, and as the end of this chapter makes very clear she is deeply apprehensive about seeing him when Lady Russell is present.

CHAPTER 14   Charles and Mary return to Uppercross. Anne accompanies Lady Russell to Bath

Charles and Mary have returned to Uppercross. Anne inquires after Captain Benwick. Charles says that he has shown lively interest in Anne; Mary denies this. The conversation moves to William Elliot, and the extraordinary coincidence of their near-encounter with him in Lyme. Lady Russell is strongly opposed to him. Anne hears that Wentworth's spirits have risen with the improvement in Louisa's condition.

The elder Musgroves return to the Great House, and their home seems filled with children. Mrs Musgrove confirms to Anne that Louisa is recovering well. But now, she learns, Wentworth has gone to Shropshire to visit his brother.

Arriving soon afterwards in Bath, Lady Russell is exhilarated by the bustle of the town; Anne, on the other hand continues to feel a deep aversion. Elizabeth has communicated the surprising news that William Elliot has been attending the family in Bath, with a determination that matches his previous reluctance.

Anne's enquiry after Benwick results in conflicting responses from Charles and from Mary. Despite the fact that Anne has in the past rejected his proposal of marriage, Charles unself-consciously tells her that Benwick intended to accompany the Musgroves, but upon learning that Anne would be three miles distant, at Kellynch, decided to defer his visit. Generously, Charles tells Anne that Benwick has made clear his admiration for her.

The Musgroves, it appears, do not feel with sufficient passion to make losses in love become obstacles to friendship.

Mary, with characteristic perversity, denies that Benwick has shown interest in Anne, and then, contradicting herself, argues that it is improper that he should evince such enthusiasm while still in mourning for Miss Harville. It is typical of Mary's insensitivity that she refers the matter to Lady Russell, who says she must see Benwick before passing judgement.

Charles indicates that he expects the young captain will find reason for visiting Kellynch before long. Mary describes him as dull and ill-bred. Anne offers an alternative view of his qualities. Point of view is making itself felt once more. Lady Russell's curiosity is aroused by the disparate evaluation. By this stage of the novel, however, we have learnt to regard her judgements with less respect than she receives from members of her circle.

At this point, Lady Russell is implacably opposed to Mr Elliot. After meeting him, however, her judgement swings to the other extreme, and in the long term she is shown to be utterly misguided. Her positive response to Bath must also count against her in our evaluation, given that Anne feels such distaste for it, and that Sir Walter and Elizabeth have settled there contentedly.

The news that Wentworth has left Lyme for Shropshire sends a signal to Anne, conflicting with an earlier indication that his own spirits were improved as a consequence of the physical recovery of Louisa Musgrove. She is now able to read that improvement as signalling alleviation of guilt, following his role in the accident, rather than the response of a devoted lover.

CHAPTER 15   **Anne takes up residence with Sir Walter and Elizabeth. They speak of the attention they have received from William Elliot. He pays an unexpected visit and there is mutual recognition between him and Anne, following their encounter at Lyme**

Happy to be able to show Anne around their dignified lodgings, and to speak of their contacts with fashionable society, her father and sister are surprisingly welcoming. Mrs Clay is more predictably cordial. Anne hears of Mr Elliot's attempts to make amends for his former neglect of the family. We learn that Elliot married a woman without prestigious social connections, but of considerable wealth and beauty. Elliot's friend, Colonel Wallis, who has been invited into their company, supplies such information, and endorses his friend's worth and good intentions.

A knock at the door, at ten in the evening, heralds the unexpected arrival of Mr Elliot. He is indeed the man encountered by Anne at Lyme. Upon recognition of her he is evidently surprised, and she is impressed by his manners and general demeanour, which appear to rival those of Wentworth. In conversation, she is struck by his 'sensible, discerning mind' (p. 156). He leaves at eleven, with Anne feeling astonished that her evening at Camden-place has been passed so pleasurably.

> Anne interprets the news from her family, making allowances for the speakers: 'She heard it all under embellishment. All that sounded extravagant or irrational in the progress of the reconciliation might have no origin but in the language of the relators' (p. 153). The effect of personal bias upon perception is a major thematic concern of *Persuasion* (see Themes). Anne is suspicious of William Elliot's motives, but concludes that he must have a genuine interest in Elizabeth. It is clear from this passage that Anne holds her elder sister in low esteem.

> Jane Austen introduces some touches of biting **satirical** humour in order to highlight the contrast between Anne's father and sister, and those admirable people, such as the Crofts and the elder Musgroves, whom she has come to know at Uppercross. Sir Walter is very taken with reports of Mrs Wallis, whom he has not met, but who is reported to possess singular physical beauty. His judgement is shaped entirely by his obsession, and has no basis in first-hand evidence.

> He has engaged in some personal research, however, and has concluded that Bath has a disproportionate number of plain women: 'once, as he had stood in a shop in Bond-street he had counted eighty-seven women go by, one after another, without there being a tolerable face among them' (p. 155). The idea of him

counting and classifying women passing by not only conjures up a ludicrous picture, but testifies to the extent of his stupidity. His life, alas, has no more serious purpose.

Anne now regards William Elliot in a highly favourable light, despite lurking suspicions that he is not entirely trustworthy. We see here that she is by no means an infallible judge of character and motive. When discussion moves to the topic of the accident in Lyme, Anne feels that Mr Elliot's perspicacity and sympathy align him with Lady Russell. As readers we may feel that this is a telling alignment. It is, of course, necessary to the development of the plot that Elliot is seen as a persuasive rival for Anne's affections. His presence on the scene helps to crystallise Wentworth's feelings, and to add urgency to his eventual declaration of love.

under-hung having a projecting lower jaw

CHAPTER 16   **Anne is concerned at the continued presence of Mrs Clay. Her father and sister court the company of Lady Dalrymple and Miss Carteret**

Anne is uneasy about the place Mrs Clay seems to occupy in the affections of her father and sister. They have entreated her to stay despite Anne's additional presence.

Sir Walter adds his voice to those commenting upon the improvement to Anne's looks. Still, Lady Russell is provoked by the undervaluing of Anne, and by the favour shown to Mrs Clay.

Sir Walter and Elizabeth are preoccupied with the arrival from Ireland of noble cousins of the family. They have become estranged from the branch of the family to which the Dowager Viscountess Dalrymple and her daughter, the Honourable Miss Carteret belong, and are anxious to repair the breach. After an exchange of letters, meetings occur.

Anne is ashamed at her father's snobbish obsequiousness, and she is unimpressed by her more distant relatives. Conversing with her on the subject, Mr Elliot insists upon the value of connections, adding that Sir Walter's preoccupation with his social superiors at least distracts him from the evidently inferior Mrs Clay. In that matter, Anne feels accord with him.

CHAPTER 16 continued

This chapter conjoins Mrs Clay and Mr Elliot as twin figures for concern. Both Anne and Lady Russell regard Mrs Clay with acute suspicion, and they are alarmed at the inability of Sir Walter and Elizabeth to recognise the threat she may pose. They fear that she is a manipulative figure, preying upon the Elliots' naivety. That suspicion acquires substance from the fact that we have seen those characteristics embodied in her father, Mr Shepherd. *Persuasion* makes a great deal of the role played by inherited qualities, passed from one generation to the next.

For Lady Russell: 'Her satisfaction in Mr Elliot outweighed all the plague of Mrs Clay' (p. 159). Anne is struck by another instance of her friend thinking differently from herself, for however pleasant her cousin appears, and however enthusiastic towards him she appeared in Chapter 15, she remains wary of his motivation.

A contrast is drawn between the snobbish pride that drives Sir Walter to court the company of the Viscountess Dalrymple, and the pride, based in a sense of family dignity, that causes Anne to deplore this wooing of acquaintance (see Theme on Pride). She hates the shallowness of her father's motives.

Mr Elliot's affirmation of the need to make useful connections reflects **ironically** on the process in which he is now involved. At an earlier stage of his life, he considered that a link to the Elliot family was of no service to him; now, he recognises certain benefits and conscientiously ingratiates himself. He joins Anne and Lady Russell in denigrating Mrs Clay, ostensibly because he disapproves of her influence. It is possible that in drawing attention to her manipulative presence, he is attempting to conceal his own.

Gowland a skin lotion, known to have been advertised in the *Bath Chronicle*

CHAPTER 17   **Anne renews acquaintance with a friend from school, who has fallen on hard times. Lady Russell foresees a marriage between Anne and William Elliot. Anne has further doubts about her cousin**

While her father and sister continue to forge a relationship with Lady Dalrymple and her daughter, Anne renews her friendship with Mrs

Smith, whom, as Miss Hamilton, she had known at school. Three years her senior, her friend comforted Anne following the death of her mother. Now, twelve years later, she is a widow, impoverished, and crippled by rheumatic fever. It is this which has driven her to take the waters at Bath. Sir Walter and Elizabeth learn of Mrs Smith's existence when Anne turns down an invitation to visit Lady Dalrymple on account of a prior arrangement to visit her schoolfriend. They express their distaste for such a connection.

Anne subsequently hears reports of a successful gathering, which included both Lady Russell and Mr Elliot. Lady Russell tells her that her cousin was most impressed by Anne's loyalty to a friend in need, and spoke of her as 'in her temper, manners, mind, a model of female excellence' (p. 171).

Lady Russell anticipates, and favours, a marriage between the two, with Anne becoming Lady Elliot, mistress of Kellynch. Anne retains her suspicions that all is not as it seems with her suave cousin.

Jane Austen's dramatic use of contrast in the service of characterisation is very evident in the distinction between Sir Walter and Elizabeth forging their connection with the Viscountess, and Anne establishing contact with Mrs Smith, a valued friend from her schooldays. Anne has nothing to gain in terms of her own material or social advancement.

She does, however, seek to profit from the lesson to be drawn from her friend's resourcefulness: she notes Mrs Smith's remarkable gift for turning a negative situation into a positive one, making the most of her lot. It is possible that Anne sees a parallel with her own efforts to profit from the pain of her own circumstances. We have seen her tendency to speak with authority on affairs of the heart, and her inclination to draw general rules from specific cases. This may be interpreted as an attempt to transform suffering into sagacity.

Sir Walter and Elizabeth regard the prospect of an acquaintance such as Mrs Smith with disdain, and her father condemns Anne's 'extraordinary taste! Every thing that revolts other people, low company, paltry rooms, foul air, disgusting associations are inviting to you' (p. 169). The abyss of sensibility that separates father and daughter is never more apparent.

Anne inherits her mother's positive qualities. This fact assumes critical importance in this chapter, on account of Lady Russell's eagerness for Anne to marry Mr Elliot, and so become in turn Lady Elliot, mistress of Kellynch-hall. His appreciation of Anne wins Lady Russell's favour; we know that she is annoyed by the neglect shown generally to the daughter who most resembles her late friend. Anne herself is charmed by the prospect of assuming her mother's place. But her more considered judgement is against accepting any proposal from Mr Elliot.

She has doubts about his character and his behaviour in the past, and suspects that a return to those ways might be possible. He seems too calculating in his efforts to please everybody:

> She prized the frank, the open-hearted, the eager character beyond all others. Warmth and enthusiasm did captivate her still. She felt that she could so much more depend upon the sincerity of those who sometimes looked or said a careless or a hasty thing, than of those whose presence of mind never varied, whose tongue never slipped. (p. 173)

Perfectly polished manners are taken to signal duplicity in this novel, where appearances rarely correspond to underlying reality. Lady Russell, significantly, can find no fault with Mr Elliot.

CHAPTER 18   **Anne receives a letter from Mary, announcing the engagement of Louisa Musgrove and Captain Benwick. She meets with the Crofts, who are visiting Bath**

After a month in Bath, Anne is eager for news of Uppercross. She knows that Henrietta has returned home, while Louisa remains at Lyme, continuing her convalescence. She receives a letter from Mary, delivered by Admiral and Mrs Croft, who are visiting Bath to seek a cure for the Admiral's gout.

A letter from Mary announces that Louisa has now returned home, and that she is to marry Captain Benwick. Anne is astonished and tries to comprehend this extraordinary development. Above all, she is exercised by the disappearance from the scene of Captain Wentworth.

When she meets the Crofts, Anne displays her customary tact and does not address the affair directly; but she discerns from their blank response that they are unaware of developments. A week or so later she encounters Admiral Croft alone, in the street. His wife has been parted from him by a blister on her heel, incurred while accompanying him on long walks, and Anne is able to talk with him as he walks home with her.

The Crofts have received, on the preceding day, a letter from Wentworth, and the Admiral shares his knowledge of Louisa's engagement to Benwick. He suggests that Wentworth should be summoned to Bath, where he might find a suitable woman to marry.

As suggested earlier, the note Anne received from Captain Wentworth, conveying news of Louisa, may actually have been written primarily to make contact with her. Comparably, the letter she now receives from Mary is to be read not for its veracity, but for the light it sheds on Mary's self-centred character, riddled with jealousy and self-pity. She is unquestionably Sir Walter's daughter, as we may see from such remarks as:

Jemima has just told me that the butcher says there is a bad sore-throat very much about. I dare say I shall catch it; and my sore-throats, you know, are always worse than anybody's. (p. 175)

Her letter was written to gloat over the fact that Captain Benwick has transferred his affections to Louisa Musgrove. Mary savours this astonishing news all the more as it allows her to pour scorn on her husband's earlier insistence that Benwick's admiration was reserved for Anne.

Jane Austen achieves an incisively satirical view of Mary through the division of her letter into two parts. The first disparages the Crofts; the second, written after they have behaved with particular respect for Mary, sings their praise. There is no constancy in her perception of others. She is interested in people only to the extent that their attitudes reflect her worth. There is a telling parallel established here with developments in Bath: Mr Elliot has courted Sir Walter and Elizabeth, and they have changed their view of him dramatically, from aloof contempt to warm approval. This is the great Elliot weakness. A more damning fact is that Lady Russell has also had a complete change of heart, although for rather more complex reasons than shallow self-obsession.

Anne tries to fathom the unanticipated match between, 'The high-spirited, joyous, talking Louisa Musgrove, and the dejected, thinking, feeling, reading Captain Benwick' (p. 177). She concludes: 'He had an affectionate heart. He must love somebody' (p. 178). Anne clearly felt no deep attachment to Benwick, and she assumes her customary role as analyst of affairs of the heart. But, she is unable to sustain the manner of detached analysis when pondering her former lover's departure: 'she thought of Captain Wentworth unshackled and free. She had some feelings which she was ashamed to investigate. They were too much like joy, senseless joy!' (p. 178). Her heart has suddenly displaced her head in governing the nature of her response to changing circumstances. (See Textual Analysis: Text 2).

The Crofts are invariably seen together; their inseparability is a measure of their loyalty and personal devotion. Mrs Croft is sufficiently selfless to walk long distances in considerable discomfort, to accompany her husband who has been ordered to walk for medical reasons. This relationship of loving mutuality contrasts with the self-centredness of Anne's family (see Theme on Selfishness and Mutuality). It also contrasts with the distance that has kept Anne and Wentworth apart, although the suggestion is increasingly that their love has in fact endured their long separation.

It is evident that the Crofts have many friends in Bath, and their sociability in public complements perfectly their preservation of an intimate privacy between themselves. In this respect, their marriage supplies a strong moral focus within *Persuasion*.

Concerned for his brother-in-law's marriage prospects, Admiral Croft asks Anne if she thinks it wise to summon him to Bath, where, despite Sir Walter's earlier protestations to the contrary, there are many pretty women. Jane Austen's **irony** is rarely more stark.

a three shilling piece these were issued by the Bank of England between 1811 and 1816, and had a lower silver content than regular shilling coinage. At 35mm across, the three shilling piece was larger than any coin currently in circulation

CHAPTER 19   **Wentworth arrives in Bath. Anne converses with him, but allows Mr Elliot to escort her home. On the next day, while walking with Lady Russell, she sees the Captain again**

It is not necessary to summon Wentworth, as he is already on his way to Bath. Later, Anne is walking in the company of Elizabeth, Mrs Clay and Mr Elliot when a rain shower causes them to take shelter in a confectioner's shop. She sees Wentworth pass by, and is flustered when, soon afterwards, he enters the shop with a group of friends. He engages her in polite conversation, despite his evident self-consciousness.

Anne is dismayed that Elizabeth snubs Wentworth before leaving to be driven home in Lady Dalrymple's carriage. Wentworth, resourcefully equipped with an umbrella, offers to accompany Anne home. She declines, as she is awaiting Mr Elliot, with whom she then departs, arm in arm. The women in Wentworth's company remark upon Elliot's good looks, and his evident attraction to his cousin. They also note Anne's prettiness, which they deem too delicate for the taste of most men.

Accompanied by her cousin, Anne finds it difficult to attend to his conversation, as she is preoccupied with Wentworth and his apparent change of heart towards her. She is confused by developments, yet there is pleasure in her agitation.

The next day, walking with Lady Russell, Anne again catches sight of Captain Wentworth, amid a group of people, on the opposite side of the road. As he approaches, she senses that Lady Russell is watching Wentworth intently, and Anne is sure she is remarking his polished appearance. Her friend, however, admits only to looking for curtains, which had been commended to her, in one of the houses. Anne is astonished at this apparent obliviousness, and is cross with herself for being distracted from Wentworth's own reaction to her passing by.

Days pass without another encounter, principally because 'the elegant stupidity of private parties' (p. 189), which preoccupies her family, situates her in a different social circle to Wentworth. She anticipates encountering him at a concert, and cancels an arrangement to visit Mrs Smith. Her loyalty in that quarter is overruled by her sense of pressing matters in another.

The meeting in Molland's shop is a significant encounter, as both Anne and Wentworth disclose through their demeanour the real resurgence of their love for one another. Her agitated response to his presence is heightened by his own evident embarrassment; Anne notes that he is blushing. If such a display of sensitivity is not entirely to be expected from a seasoned naval officer, the formal restraint with which he conducts a conversation with Anne is in keeping with what we know of Wentworth's customary composure. Once again, Jane Austen is highlighting a disparity between the surface and the depths of character.

The disdain with which Elizabeth Elliot treats Captain Wentworth is strikingly different from the warmth which is now extended by her to her cousin, William. As we now recognise that these two men are manoeuvring to become suitors for Anne, the favour displayed by Elizabeth appears as an inverse assessment of their actual worthiness to marry her sister. Anne is hurt by Elizabeth's behaviour, largely because it recalls the Elliot snobbishness which formed the context for the termination of her engagement to Wentworth.

Following the departure of Anne with William Elliot, Wentworth's circle discuss their apparent suitability as a couple, and remark upon Anne's delicacy of appearance. It is acknowledged that such a quality is to be appreciated only by a man of real discrimination; we should recognise that Wentworth is such a man.

Lady Russell's apparent preoccupation with curtains, while Anne's attention is concentrated on the proximity of Wentworth, is another striking contrast. We may feel that we are being led again to doubt the alleged perspicacity of Lady Russell, diverted by fashion from a matter of great importance to her purported favourite. Or we may regard this as an underestimation of Lady Russell, and choose to see her apparent obliviousness to Wentworth as a deliberate act of exclusion, to suspect that she is aware of him, but opts to ignore his presence. Either way, Jane Austen is showing how obsession frames perception: Anne's mind is focused upon her former lover, and her consciousness of him becomes acute; Lady Russell is distracted by a temporary, and altogether less weighty concern with curtains.

Anne desires to talk with Wentworth; 'she felt that she owed him attention' (p. 189). This formulation casts a light of selflessness across the wish to see him, although it is surely a measure of what Anne needs for her own peace of mind. This perception of a form of self-interest, underlying her expression of debt to Wentworth, is granted further substance when she decides to cancel an appointment to visit Mrs Smith. Her friendship for this unfortunate woman has featured as an index of Anne's altruism. Giving precedence to a concert, which the Captain is likely to attend, seems to confirm that obligation is being overruled by passion in this instance.

Molland's the *Bath Directory* for 1812 records this establishment, at 2 Milsom Street, as owned by a cook and confectioner

CHAPTER 20   Sir Walter, Elizabeth, Anne, and Mrs Clay attend a concert. Wentworth is there, and converses with Anne. She senses his increasing warmth towards her, although he reverts to formality after seeing her with William Elliot. In the course of the concert Elliot expresses his wish to marry her

Sir Walter, his daughters, and Mrs Clay arrive early at the concert rooms. Awaiting Lady Dalrymple, they are approached by Captain Wentworth. Stepping away from her group, Anne greets him. Their conversation turns to the accident at Lyme, and to the subsequent good fortune of Benwick's relationship with Louisa Musgrove. Anne says she would like to revisit Lyme.

Lady Dalrymple arrives, and Anne recognises that she is obliged to join the family group. Despite being separated from Wentworth, she is uplifted by her new understanding of their situation. Seated beside

Mr Elliot, Anne derives considerable pleasure from the evening's entertainment.

Her cousin praises her accomplishments and decries her modesty. He also reveals that he has known of her by repute for many years, although he declines to disclose the source of his information. He does, however, express his wish that Anne should remain an Elliot, an evident declaration of his intentions towards her. At the same time, she overhears Lady Dalrymple, in conversation with her father, praising Wentworth's good looks. This combination of factors causes her to wish she could escape from her cousin's attentions. During the second half of the concert, William Elliot moves elsewhere, but she remains apart from Captain Wentworth.

Eventually, Wentworth approaches her again, but his attitude has reverted to its former formality. Just as he is becoming more relaxed, Mr Elliot intervenes, requesting that Anne should translate some Italian lyrics for Miss Carteret. Unwillingly, she allows politeness to draw her away. Wentworth departs shortly afterwards, with a discomposed farewell.

> Wentworth and Anne discuss the startling alliance of Louisa Musgrove and Captain Benwick. They had, of course, been popularly perceived as their own potential respective partners. After initially welcoming the match, Wentworth registers surprise at the suddenness with which his friend transferred his affections from the late, and most worthy, Fanny Harville. We noted earlier that Anne might be seen to have a morbid affinity with Fanny, and here she recognises, with gratitude and excitement, that Wentworth seems to speak from his own experience of trying to recover from his love for Anne, who has been lost to him.

> Referring to Louisa's accident, Wentworth says: 'It had been my doing – solely mine. She would not have been obstinate if I had not been weak' (p. 193). He had succumbed to persuasion of a kind that proved nearly disastrous, erring on the side of risk rather than caution.

> Anne remarks that she has travelled little – a situation that might of course have been remedied if, like Mrs Croft, she had married

a sailor. Feminist critics have shown considerable interest in *Persuasion*'s portrayal of the lack of freedom to move or act independently, which women of Anne Elliot's class endured (see Contemporary Approaches). Jane Austen herself led a life that was strictly delimited in geographical terms, while her brothers in the navy travelled extensively.

Anne comments that her recollections of Lyme are 'very agreeable' (p. 193), a thinly veiled comment on her recognition there of clear signs that Wentworth's passion for her was reawakening. Her wish to return there may be taken as a tacit reciprocation of his interest in her.

Anne is aware that 'he had a heart returning to her'; in short, 'He must love her' (p. 195). Her consequent elation is contrasted with the happiness felt by her sister, Elizabeth, on account of her appearance in public alongside the prestigious Miss Carteret. The narrator distinguishes their joy: 'the origin of one all selfish vanity, of the other all generous attachment' (p. 194). The distinction is comparable to that made earlier between the pride which makes Anne feel repulsion towards her father's efforts to ingratiate himself with Lady Dalrymple, and the shallow pride in social connection which motivates him to that ingratiation (see Theme on Pride).

Anne now has little doubt that Wentworth's love has been fully rekindled, but the presence of William Elliot complicates matters. His conversation suggests that he hopes to marry Anne, and she becomes alarmed at the possibility that his proximity might persuade Wentworth that his feelings are not reciprocated. It is important to note here that Anne has no right to propose marriage to Wentworth; she must await his proposal, while signalling her interest in him, within the bounds of decorum. Such signs are always subject to possible misinterpretation. The intensity of her emotions is captured in the concluding hyperbolic declaration: 'It was misery to think of Mr Elliot's attentions. – Their evil was incalculable' (p. 199).

Miss Larolles a talkative character in Fanny Burney's *Cecilia* (1782)

CHAPTER 21   **Anne visits Mrs Smith, who discloses her former acquaintance with William Elliot, and reveals that he is self-centred and ill-intentioned**

Next morning, Anne recalls her promise to visit Mrs Smith. She discusses the previous evening's concert with her friend. It is soon evident that Mrs Smith, from another source, has acquired more information about the audience than Anne possesses. Anne was there, but was distracted. Her friend observes that Anne's face betrays that she conversed last evening with the person she found 'the most agreeable in the world' (p. 201).

But Mrs Smith's conversation shifts to Mr Elliot; it is apparent that she thinks he is the person Anne loves. She confides that she has known Elliot in the past, and that she now requires his assistance. Anne insists that although she respects her cousin, she does not love him, and she will not marry him. Mrs Smith reveals that her supposition is founded in gossip, brought to her by her nurse, from the wife of Colonel Wallis.

Anne presses Mrs Smith to speak of her former close acquaintance with William Elliot. Persuaded that she must tell the truth, she announces:

> Mr Elliot is a man without heart or conscience; a designing, wary, cold-blooded being, who thinks only of himself; who, for his own interest or ease, would be guilty of any cruelty, or any treachery, that could be perpetrated without risk of his general character. He has no feeling for others. Those whom he has been the chief cause of leading into ruin, he can neglect and desert without the smallest compunction. He is totally beyond the reach of any sentiment of justice or compassion. Oh! he is black at heart, hollow and black! (p. 206)

Anne is astonished at the outburst.

Mrs Smith explains that Elliot was a friend of her husband prior to their marriage, and she came to know him as a member of their intimate social circle. It was from Mrs Smith that Elliot received those glowing reports of Anne, which left a lasting impression in his mind. She explains that he had entered into marriage with a social inferior, the daughter of a grazier, and granddaughter of a butcher. Despite her humble origins, the woman had considerable wealth, and the marriage granted the young Elliot easy access to money and the independence it brings.

Mrs Smith produces a letter written by Elliot to her late husband. In it, he expresses his contempt for Sir Walter in forceful terms, and regrets that he should himself have Walter as his second name. Anne is upset by the disrespectful comments, and is uneasy at her own violation of private correspondence. Mrs Smith then affirms that Elliot is quite sincere in his desire to marry Anne. She has testimony to this, indirectly, from Colonel Wallis, via her nurse.

Mrs Smith refers to Mrs Clay, and her supposed intention to become Sir Walter's wife. She reports that William Elliot, having developed an interest in accession to the baronetcy, which he conspicuously lacked as a young man, is alarmed at reports of this unwelcome intrusion. Elliot has determined to renew acquaintance with the family, and to ensure that he will become Sir William without undue impediment.

Mrs Smith indicates that Elliot's influence hastened the financial ruin of her husband, the extent of which became apparent only after his death. Elliot was named executor for Smith's will, but he treated that duty and his friend's wife with indifference. She is particularly aggrieved because her husband had financial interests in the West Indies, which might be activated to her considerable benefit. But she cannot act and Elliot has failed to do so on her behalf. It was in this quarter that Mrs Smith had hoped to engage Anne's assistance, when she believed marriage to her cousin to be inevitable.

The meeting ends with Anne securing Mrs Smith's permission to convey the truth about William Elliot to Lady Russell.

Anne's visit to Mrs Smith is not entirely altruistic; after postponing the meeting in order to see Wentworth, she now welcomes the engagement as it will enable her to avoid encountering Mr Elliot. Jane Austen is not presenting an entirely idealised heroine in Anne; like the other characters, to varying degrees, she is vulnerable to the influence of self-interest.

We see a very different Anne Elliot at this stage of *Persuasion*. Her elevated mood constitutes a lens of romance that enhances the world around her:

Prettier musings of high-wrought love and eternal constancy, could never have passed along the streets of Bath, than Anne was sporting with from Camden-place to Westgate-buildings. It was almost enough to spread purification and perfume all the way. (p. 200)

Anne's rose-coloured view of the world contrasts tellingly with the dark mood that frames her perception of William Elliot at the end of the preceding chapter. In her conversation with Mrs Smith, Anne hears an equally condemnatory assessment of her cousin's character. It astonishes her despite her own comparable outburst. Now her mood has altered radically, while her friend's view of Elliot is charged with the sense of wrong she has suffered at his hands. Our judgement of others is never a simple matter of objective evaluation. As Mrs Smith remarks later in this chapter, 'self will intrude' (p. 214) (see Theme on Selfishness and Mutuality).

Mrs Smith's revelations concerning William Elliot's marriage introduce direct reference to an important dimension of social history that illuminates many of the political assumptions that underlie Jane Austen's fiction. Mrs Elliot's family were from the lower social orders. Since the Middle Ages, until relatively recently, the English class structure had remained unchanged. Jane Austen's allegiance is to the aristocracy and the gentry, the controlling stratum of the old order. But her age saw significant shifts of power away from that class, and a marked increase in upward mobility from the lower classes (see Historical Background on The Changing Nature of Society).

The conversation also introduces reference to the colonial trade in the West Indies, which brought wealth to many members of the rising mercantile class, but involved exploitation of human communities remote from Somersetshire (see Contemporary Approaches: Post-Colonial).

Listening to Mrs Smith, Anne comes to recognise that 'Mr Elliot is evidently a disingenuous, artificial, worldly man, who has never had any better principle to guide him than selfishness' (p. 214). It might be added that it is a family trait, from which she is largely preserved through her resemblance to her mother. A key question in *Persuasion* is, at what point does inevitable self-interest become inexcusable selfishness?

Mrs Smith seems like a good friend, but just as Anne forewent an agreed visit in order to further her own ends, so her friend seems quite content to sanction Anne's marriage when it appears it will help her financially, but is scathing about the man when she knows that approval will not assist her own needs. Anne asks how her friend could have offered such a warm endorsement of so cruel a figure, when the marriage had seemed likely. Mrs Smith says feebly that she conceived no alternative but to speak well of him.

The contrast between her self-serving malleability, and those determined forces of persuasion which had terminated Anne's romance with Wentworth eight years before could scarcely be stronger. Anne considers with horror the possibility that she might have married her cousin: 'It was just possible that she might have been persuaded by Lady Russell!' (p. 216).

CHAPTER 22   **William Elliot visits Sir Walter and his family. He declares his intention to leave Bath for a few days, but is later seen in conversation with Mrs Clay. Charles and Mary, Henrietta and her mother, and Captain Harville arrive in Bath. While Anne is with them, they are joined by Wentworth**

At home, Anne considers the implications of her new knowledge concerning her cousin. William Elliot had called during her absence, and returns to visit the family that evening. Anne treats him with studied coolness. He announces that he will be away from Bath for two days.

Next morning, Anne prepares to visit Lady Russell to seek her advice. Sir Walter and Elizabeth speak of Lady Russell with some condescension. Then, to the surprise of all, Charles and Mary Musgrove arrive. They bring with them Mrs Musgrove, Henrietta, and Captain Harville. We learn that Charles Hayter's fortunes have improved sufficiently to enable his marriage to Henrietta to proceed, and that Louisa has now recovered well, although she seems a much more subdued young woman.

Anne postpones the visit to Lady Russell in order to renew her acquaintance with the group from Uppercross. Wentworth joins them, and Anne is anxious that the accord in their desires should become apparent, although she is reluctant to signal her love for him explicitly. Mary draws her attention to Mr Elliot, whom they can see from a window, still, unexpectedly, in Bath, and in conversation, curiously, with Mrs Clay.

Charles tells his mother that he has booked a box at the theatre, for nine people, for the following evening. Mary is angry, as this clashes with a party to which they have been invited, at her father's house. Charles is indifferent to the party, but Mary is keen to meet Lady Dalrymple, and William Elliot. The conciliatory Mrs Musgrove suggests that theatre-going should be arranged for another day. Anne concurs, although taking the opportunity to say that the party holds no attraction for her. In this way she hopes to indicate to Wentworth that Elliot has no influence over her feelings.

A brief exchange – emotionally charged, yet superficially restrained – occurs between Wentworth and Anne. Henrietta Musgrove interrupts, and then Sir Walter and Elizabeth arrive, bringing with them, Anne feels, 'a general chill' and 'an instant oppression' (p. 230). Her mortification at their attitude is mollified somewhat by an evident warming towards Captain Wentworth, whom Elizabeth now recognises as a potential social asset.

To Anne's astonishment, Elizabeth extends an invitation to Wentworth, before she and her father depart. Anne is filled with nervous anticipation, wondering whether the Captain will attend the Elliot soirée. She does have sufficient presence of mind, however, to challenge Mrs Clay concerning her encounter with Mr Elliot, who was supposed to have left Bath. Mrs Clay appears guilty, and offers a flustered explanation.

Anne is glad to comprehend the actuality of William Elliot's situation, but characteristically she feels concern for the impact the revelation will have on Lady Russell, and on her own family. She is sensitive to the contexts within which truth becomes apparent, and knows that shifts in understanding of motive have ramifications for human relationships.

Ironically, Mrs Clay declares that William Elliot's relationship to Sir Walter has developed to resemble that of a son to his father. Her admiration for Elliot seems entirely contrary to the logic of the situation recently disclosed to Anne. When Elliot returns, Anne is acutely conscious of his insincerity. She adjusts her response to him accordingly, although she does not wish to alert him to his being discovered. She considers that he and Mrs Clay differ only in the degree of their hypocrisy.

The change wrought in Louisa Musgrove as a product of her suffering might be regarded as a parallel in physical terms to the change that occurred following Anne's psychological injury on the termination of her engagement.

The conversation between William Elliot and Mrs Clay, witnessed by Mary and Anne, is a strange development, but it culminates the strands within the novel which have linked the two figures despite their ostensible animosity. The discussion, which they wished to keep clandestine, is another instance of appearance being an unreliable guide to truth.

It is evident that as Anne becomes able to admit to herself the love she feels towards Wentworth, her attitude towards her father and Elizabeth becomes increasingly dismissive. In contrast to the authenticity of her own emotions, she becomes intensely sensitive to their 'heartless elegance' (p. 230).

dab chick another name for the little grebe, a diving water-bird

CHAPTER 23   **At the White Hart Inn, Anne talks with Harville about Benwick's apparent inconstancy, while Wentworth writes a letter nearby. Wentworth gives a note to Anne, declaring his enduring devotion to her. Soon afterwards, as he walks her home, the mutuality of their love is finally established**

Anne's commitment to attend the Musgroves results in further deferral of her planned visit to Lady Russell. At their lodgings in the White Hart Inn, she encounters Wentworth, with Captain Harville, composing a letter. Mary and Henrietta have gone shopping, so Anne is left to overhear Mrs Musgrove's account to Mrs Croft of her daughter's engagement.

The discussion makes Anne self-conscious about her own past and her present situation, and glancing in the Captain's direction, she finds that he has stopped writing to take 'one quick, conscious look at her' (p. 235). Next, she notices Harville, who has moved to stand by a window, gesturing for her to join him.

He shows her a portrait of Benwick, executed for Fanny Harville, but now intended as a gift for Louisa Musgrove. Harville confides to Anne his view that his sister would not have forgotten Benwick so quickly as he has apparently come to terms with her loss. Anne, characteristically, derives from this instance a general rule about the relative capacities of men and women to recover from such loss (see Textual Analysis: Text 3). Wentworth continues to write a letter on Harville's behalf, but at one point he drops his pen, and it is evident that he has overheard and drawn personal significance from this conversation.

Harville speaks of the feelings of naval men, on leaving and subsequently on returning to their families. Anne does not doubt their depth of feeling, but claims for women the privilege 'of loving longest, when existence or when hope is gone' (p. 238).

Mrs Croft takes her leave. Wentworth has finished the letter and seems keen to depart, also. He leaves the room, only to return a moment later, in order to collect his gloves, and to pass a letter to Anne 'with eyes of glowing entreaty' (p. 239). It contains an impassioned statement of his devotion, and requests some indication as to whether his feelings are reciprocated.

Anne is overcome. Her discomfiture is apparent to the returning members of the company, who surround her and show her animated concern, which she finds most unwelcome. Charles Musgrove undertakes to accompany Anne home, but *en route* they encounter Wentworth, and Musgrove surrenders his charge to the Captain. In the ensuing scene, it is perfectly clear that the couple's commitment of eight and a half years earlier has been renewed. Together, they trace the resurgence of their love through the events of the preceding weeks.

The conversation between Mrs Musgrove and Mrs Croft returns our attention to the novel's thematic tension between risk and caution (see Theme on Risk and Caution). These women have been characterised as sensible and reliable, and both have entered into notably successful marriages. Both abhor long engagements, which involve an over-cautious deferral of pleasure and responsibility. Yet both recognise the need for parents to be sure that material means will be available to support a marriage in the long term. This is, of course, immediately pertinent to Henrietta's engagement to Hayter, but has obvious relevance to Anne's situation.

We have come to suspect that Lady Russell's counsel was driven by her own snobbish distaste for Wentworth, and by her over-zealous concern for Anne. But a case is now made for the necessity of prudence, which might reconcile us to an element of wisdom in Lady Russell's advice. Overhearing the discussion, Anne is clearly able to relate its substance to her own engagement, particularly as she is keenly aware of Wentworth's proximity.

In his conversation with Anne, Harville refers to literature for evidence of the fickleness of women and the constancy of men. He is aware that Anne is devoted to reading, and he anticipates that she will acknowledge the authority of writers. But he also acknowledges that most books have been written by men, and Anne readily takes this up:

Men have had every advantage of us in telling their own story. Education has been theirs in so much higher a degree; the pen has been in their hands. I will not allow books to prove any thing. (p. 237)

Jane Austen would clearly have enjoyed this **ironic** reflection upon her own practice (see Textual Analysis: Text 3). More generally, this observation may be seen as a criticism of the social injustice that extended so many favours to men of the upper and middle classes, while confining and delimiting women (see Contemporary Approaches: Feminism).

Anne continues by concluding that:

It is a difference of opinion which does not admit of proof. We each begin probably with a little bias towards our own sex, and upon that bias build every circumstance in favour of it which has occurred within our own circle. (p. 237)

This may weaken the force of her criticism as an anticipation of later feminist arguments, but it does align with a major thematic concern of *Persuasion*: the fact that point of view and personal preoccupations invariably condition perception and comprehension (see Theme on Personal Bias and Point of View).

The discussion with Harville presents us with a lengthy sequence of dialogue; we overhear direct speech between him and Anne. The length of that conversation arguably leaves us more ready to accept the subsequent reconciliation of Anne with Wentworth in indirectly reported form, rather than through direct representation in dialogue. Jane Austen was well aware of the difficulties of trying to capture an emotionally charged scene through direct speech, and she opted to rely upon such narratorial assertion as: 'Her character was now fixed on his mind as perfection itself, maintaining the loveliest medium of fortitude and gentleness' (p. 244).

This technique also has the benefit of delimiting variations in our response; in a novel which often invites us to assume a sceptical role as interpreters of character and action, it is important at this point to affirm unequivocally the worth of Anne Elliot and of Frederick Wentworth, and to confirm the desirability of their reconciliation.

Direct speech is reintroduced as, the passion of the moment having subsided, the couple trace the events of previous weeks in order to chart the course of their revived love. It is important for Jane Austen that their emotion is seen to be grounded in gradual recognition of one another's worth, rather than being merely a matter of unthinking arousal of passionate feelings.

One of the issues investigated by this novel is the practicability of deriving lessons from experience. It is evidence of the couple's worthiness that they are capable of such insight. From the incident at Lyme, Wentworth has learnt:

to distinguish between the steadiness of principle and the obstinacy of self-will, between the darings of heedlessness and the resolution of a collected mind. There, he had seen every thing to exalt in his estimation the woman he has lost, and there begun to deplore the pride, the folly, the madness of resentment, which had kept him from trying to regain her when thrown in his way. (p. 244)

Wentworth also recognises the foolish pride which prevented him writing to Anne years earlier, when his fortunes had begun to increase.

Pride takes different forms in this book, as we have seen. It can be beneficial, as is the case with Anne's pride in struggling to preserve her family's dignity. It can also be harmful, as in Sir Walter's incorrigible snobbery. Wentworth can now see his own pride as falling within the latter category.

Acts of persuasion also appear in differing lights. Wentworth, seeing Anne in company with Lady Russell, inevitably perceived 'the indelible, immoveable impression of what persuasion had once done' (p. 246). Anne, on the other hand, while acknowledging the damage done by unsound advice, affirms that she was right to follow the advice of Lady Russell, who stood in place of a mother to her, and so required her dutiful response: 'If I was wrong in yielding to persuasion once, remember that it was to persuasion exerted on the side of safety, not of risk' (p. 246).

the Sultaness Scheherazade's head in the *Arabian Nights Entertainments*, Scheherazade kept beheading at bay through her capacity to tell stories

CHAPTER 24   **Anne Elliot and Captain Wentworth are married**

The narrator makes a direct first-person address to readers, affirming that all now followed as it must: Anne and Wentworth overcame all objections, and their marriage was recorded in the 'Baronetage', in Sir Walter Elliot's own handwriting.

Lady Russell, who distrusted Wentworth and favoured William Elliot, has the difficult task of overcoming her prejudices and admitting her error. She soon learns to appreciate the Captain's true worth.

Mary is content with her sister's alliance. Elizabeth remains unattached, disappointed by the withdrawal from the scene of Mr Elliot. Mrs Clay followed him to London, and it is later learnt that she has become a member of his household. Sir Walter shared his daughter's surprise at this turn of events, consoled only partially by their acquaintance with Lady Dalrymple.

Anne has limited company to add to her new husband's acquaintance: Lady Russell and Mrs Smith. Through the Captain's good offices the latter attains her West Indian legacy.

The novel concludes:

> Anne was tenderness itself, and she had the full worth of it in Captain
> Wentworth's affection. His profession was all that could ever make her friends
> wish that tenderness less; the dread of a future war all that could dim her sunshine.
> She gloried in being a sailor's wife, but she must pay the tax of quick alarm for
> belonging to that profession which is, if possible, more distinguished in its
> domestic virtues than in its national importance. (pp. 253–4)

Anne's marriage is entered into Sir Walter's copy of the 'Baronetage'. This recalls the beginning of the novel, and we recognise a final seal of approval.

It is rather startling, especially given Anne's remarks at the end of the preceding chapter, to be confronted with the stark assertion that, 'There was nothing less for Lady Russell to do, than to admit that she had been pretty completely wrong, and to take up a new set of opinions and of hopes' (p. 251). Yet, the wisdom of this woman has been referred to repeatedly throughout the novel.

As readers, we have been granted insights all along which have hinted at the limitations of her judgement, but it is nonetheless surprising to encounter so absolute a dismissal. Is Jane Austen adding a further touch of **irony** to our perception of this character? It seems clear that Lady Russell's real affection for Anne helps her to overcome her wounded pride, and that is to her credit. Soon, she experiences 'little hardship in attaching herself as a mother to the man who was securing the happiness of her other child' (p. 251). It is difficult to be stringently critical of Lady Russell when she is presented in these terms.

Wentworth's intervention to assist Mrs Smith in securing her husband's legacy of property in the West Indies would undoubtedly have appeared to contemporary readers as an unequivocal act of kindness. Today, we cannot fail to recognise in that legacy an implied system of colonial exploitation. The wealth and comfort of her class was dependent upon the oppression of people overseas (see Contemporary Approaches: Post-Colonial).

The concluding sentences affirm the positive worth of Anne Elliot's 'tenderness', while suggesting that excessive sensitivity and excessive attachment are not wise given the uncertainties of life. This is especially the case as Anne is married to a naval officer, whose profession involves risk. This defence of moderation is characteristic of the values found in Jane Austen's fiction. The conclusion is also a sincerely felt statement of praise and thanks to the navy which had defended England so effectively throughout the recent Napoleonic wars (see Historical Background on The War against Napoleon).

PART THREE

CRITICAL APPROACHES

CHARACTERISATION

It is essential to recognise that Jane Austen's characterisation in *Persuasion* does not achieve its effects through consideration of individuals in isolation. Rather, each character is presented in a set of relationships to others, and we arrive at our sense of them largely through comparative evaluation. In other words, we are able to note similarities and contrasts in the way characters behave in comparable situations.

Of course, Anne Elliot is central to the way we read the novel, and the narrator allows us far greater access to her feelings and perceptions than to those of other characters. Nonetheless, we are rarely invited to consider her in isolation. It will be instructive to consider briefly how our understanding of some of the other characters affects our understanding of the heroine.

SIR WALTER ELLIOT

As the first character we encounter, Sir Walter leaves a lasting impression. Much is made in *Persuasion* of inherited characteristics. The vanity and snobbishness which shape every aspect of Sir Walter's behaviour are equally evident in the characterisation of his daughters, Elizabeth and Mary. We are soon aware that Anne has escaped this inheritance, and although her mother is not physically present in the novel, her admirable qualities are embodied in Anne's virtues.

Persuasion is concerned with the ways in which our actions are determined by personal bias or prejudice. Sir Walter's twin obsessions – rank and beauty – have played a material role in preventing Anne's marriage to Wentworth. They are markers of his taste, which is easily recognised as shallow and unthinking. The only reflection that matters to Sir Walter is his own, seen in the many mirrors which furnish his rooms. In a comical passage, Admiral Croft announces that he has put the looking-glasses in storage, which heightens our sense of Sir Walter's foolishness by contrast with the practical good sense of the estimable Croft.

Sir Walter is a comic figure, and that contrasts with the melancholy fate which has befallen Anne. But the humour is often savage. Jane Austen was **satirising** the foibles of a circle of shallow individuals. There is little in the humorous characterisation of the owner of Kellynch-hall that makes him palatable. He is basically despicable, and in consequence Anne lives in near isolation. The desperate nature of such isolation becomes entirely apparent at the conclusion, when her marriage to Wentworth brings only two friends into his acquaintance: Mrs Smith, a friend only recently rediscovered after years of separation, and Lady Russell, who played so large a role in terminating the earlier engagement which would have brought timely expansion to her social horizons.

LADY RUSSELL

Appropriate interpretation of this character poses a real challenge, as she is revealed to us in a manner that is far from straightforward. In fact, the moral **ambiguities** within *Persuasion* are focused in Lady Russell. Conventionally, within her social circle, she is regarded as a font of wisdom, a reliable source of measured sagacity. But throughout the narration we are given indications that her judgement is often deeply flawed, and that her perception of events is regularly distorted by a snobbishness which aligns her with Sir Walter, rather than with Anne Elliot.

In her favour, she discerns the worth of Anne and deplores the neglect she endures from her family. A crucial fact is that Lady Russell was an intimate friend of Lady Elliot, Anne's mother. She confirms that Anne resembles her mother, and shares her admirable traits. There are also indications that relations between Lady Russell and Sir Walter are rather cooler than is initially indicated, and at times we are invited to conclude that her real interest in the family resides solely with Anne.

In that light we might view her acts of persuasion towards ending Anne's engagement as examples of genuine affection, in keeping with a maternal role. At the end of the novel, we are even invited to believe that she has come to regard Wentworth as a son-in-law.

On the debit side, her taste for Bath, and her insensitivity to Anne's reasons for feeling uncomfortable there suggest shallowness. Her change of heart with regard to William Elliot is further evidence of a blinkered awareness that confounds the popularly held view of her perspicacity.

Lady Russell is a complex amalgam of strengths and weaknesses, and if we remain at the end uncertain of our response to her, then we have taken on board Jane Austen's implied advice that clear-cut judgements are by no means always appropriate.

ELIZABETH ELLIOT

The eldest of Sir Walter's daughters functions as yet another mirror to accompany him on his daily round. She is so similar to him in all respects that Sir Walter cannot fail to take great pleasure in her presence. They are inseparable, but not because they care for one another as Admiral and Mrs Croft do. Rather they are united in self-centredness.

Early in the novel Elizabeth Elliot's character is encapsulated when her suggested acts of retrenchment include termination of some charitable donations, and refraining from taking a present to her sister, Anne. At the end of *Persuasion*, we are not surprised to learn that she remains unmarried. Her obsession with her own and her father's appearance and status precludes that mutuality upon which enduring relationships are necessarily founded.

MARY ELLIOT

We see more of Mary than of Elizabeth, but they are markedly similar characters. Despite being married to Charles Musgrove, Mary exhibits no feelings of warmth towards him, and he seems to tolerate her rather than exhibit real affection. He is not an introspective character, and finds comfort in field sports, which offer him pleasures not to be rivalled at home. It is hinted that he might have developed into a more estimable human being if Anne had been willing to marry him.

Mary is not only a poor wife, she is also a terrible mother. Her inadequacy in that role is highlighted through contrast with Anne's resourcefulness in looking after little Charles, and with Anne's subsequent attention to the injured Louisa Musgrove. Such acts of caring are alien to the selfish Mary, but central to Anne's outlook on life.

Mary's maternal ineptness might be seen to cast in a more positive light Lady Russell's aspiration to act as a surrogate mother for Anne.

LOUISA AND HENRIETTA MUSGROVE

Admiral Croft says he is unable to tell these amiable young women apart, and that passing remark condemns them even as it praises them. The sisters are pleasant and lively, they are unobjectionable, but entirely unexceptional. Lady Russell experiences vicious pleasure when she believes that Wentworth, who once appreciated the superior Anne Elliot, has fallen in love with Louisa Musgrove.

Louisa's vivacity provides a telling contrast to the constrained and visibly diminished condition of twenty-seven-year-old Anne. The incident in Lyme is a pivotal point in the plot, and a revelatory moment for Wentworth who recognises the value of caution and the dangers of impetuousity.

It is to Henrietta's credit that when the sisters are vying for the attentions of Captain Wentworth she accedes to Louisa's persuasion, and acknowledges her ongoing commitment to Charles Hayter. That relationship elucidates Anne's position eight years earlier, in that it depends for its development upon the young curate's material advancement. It was exactly that consideration which had crucially determined the fate of Anne's engagement.

MRS SMITH

Mrs Smith occupies a curious role in the novel, and like Lady Russell she is not a straightforward character to interpret. It is perhaps no coincidence that she also took on a kind of maternal role with regard to Anne, when they met at school, shortly after Lady Elliot's death. Anne has deemed both women worthy of her friendship, but that approval should be considered in relation to the limited choice of friends available to her.

It is revealed that Mrs Smith entered into fashionable society, and there are hints of excessive indulgence quite contrary to Anne's taste for moderation. Her subsequent illness and decline provides Anne with further opportunity to demonstrate her caring nature, although that is tellingly compromised when she allows her sense of obligation to her old friend to be subordinated to her desire to attend a concert at which Wentworth will be present. Her passions at that point override her conscience. Anne is rescued from appearing an idealised paragon.

MR AND MRS MUSGROVE, THE CROFTS, THE HARVILLES

These three examples of successful marriage render acute Anne's awareness of what she has lost through succumbing to persuasion, and breaking her engagement to Wentworth. Their hospitality, openness, and generosity highlight through contrast the qualities missing from Anne's own experience of family and home. The togetherness of the Crofts is heart-warming and is in poignant contrast to the separation endured by Anne and Wentworth.

WILLIAM WALTER ELLIOT

William Elliot is revealed as a ruthless opportunist. The mercenary nature of his first marriage is indicative, and is also a travesty of the emotional commitment which eventually leads to Anne's marriage. His concerted efforts at manipulation of the Elliot family are an intensified version of the ostensibly more benign manipulation we have seen earlier in the novel from Mr Shepherd and Lady Russell.

The lawyer arranged the letting of Kellynch-hall, with evident self-interest, and his daughter's continued presence is a reminder of his influence in Sir Walter's affairs. The evident complicity of Mrs Clay with William Elliot hints at a substantial conspiracy, although its full nature is never made explicit.

William Elliot is proof that manners can deceive, and the fact that he dupes Lady Russell so entirely is important to our view of her. Anne responds to those signals she has been taught to respect, but she retains a suspicion that Mr Elliot is not to be trusted. In part this may be intuition, but it also shows her capacity to remember the past, and to derive lessons from Elliot's former behaviour.

FREDERICK WENTWORTH

Wentworth has all the attributes of a dashing hero of romance, but like Anne he is preserved from that perfection which would preclude him from being a credible human being. He acknowledges at the end that his pride has prevented an earlier reconciliation with Anne, and there are numerous instances in the novel of his efforts to keep that pride intact. Eventually, of course, it is overwhelmed by his love for her.

The couple share certain characteristics, such as compassion, resourcefulness, loyalty, and discretion, which distinguish them as superior figures, and make their marriage an appropriate outcome to the novel. He is Mrs Croft's brother, and although she appears an altogether more homely figure, her good-heartedness and simple honesty may be taken as a positive indication of her brother's nature.

The fact that Wentworth is a naval officer would have ensured his popularity amongst contemporary readers, who had good reason to be grateful to that service following the recent wars against Napoleon's France. It also establishes him as a self-reliant professional man who has taken risks and has won social advancement and considerable wealth.

ANNE ELLIOT

In a letter to her niece, Jane Austen expressed her fears that Anne Elliot was 'almost too good'. But she is not so good that she does not invite our sympathy. It is soon evident that she is a victim, primarily of her father's foolishness, and that she has been condemned to a confined existence. Typically, Jane Austen gives little direct description of Anne's features, but we know that she is a delicately attractive woman, who has suffered some loss of her looks due to the traumatic experience of backing away from marriage to the man she loves. At twenty-seven, she is markedly older than the conventional heroines of popular romance.

In large part she is characterised through comparison, either explicit or implied, with the flaws of others, but her worthiness is also highlighted by acts of kindness and by her unselfish capacity to be useful, especially in a crisis. She is sensitive and intelligent, so not only does she befriend the grieving Captain Benwick, but she engages him in critical discussion of literature. She is later able to translate Italian song lyrics, for the benefit of her cousin.

Such accomplishments have been acquired despite her family's philistinism, but she is undemonstrative about them. There are moments when she does appear to act out of character; notably, her deferral of an arranged visit to Mrs Smith. More noteworthy is Anne's tendency to draw general moral conclusions from particular instances of human behaviour. This is by no means necessarily a negative capability, indeed it may be considered admirable, but it does result in occasional observations that have a detachment which seems almost callous.

It is as if Anne's own suffering has led to a kind of numbing of her sensitivity through the introduction of critical distance. Arguably, it also reflects the mentoring influence of Lady Russell, who has a similar tendency to sit in aloof judgement. It seems likely that Anne's very limited experience of the world is also a contributory factor to this tendency to make large statements. If it is indeed a learnt characteristic, we may assume that her new circumstances and broader horizons at the end of the novel will soften her tone.

THEMES

ECONOMY AND EXTRAVAGANCE

The plot of *Persuasion* derives its initial momentum from the fact that Sir Walter Elliot is forced to retrench, and so quit Kellynch-hall for temporary residence in Bath. The retrenchment is a consequence of the baronet's failure to match his expenditure to his income. His inability to be moderate is one aspect of his evident foolishness. With **Augustan** assurance, Jane Austen assumes that her readers will accept moderation as a virtue, and will recognise the lamentable consequences of excess.

Sir Walter's extravagance is ironic, given the fact that eight years earlier Anne had been pressed to give up Wentworth because he could not guarantee financial security. Lady Russell is again pressed into service to advise economy. Anne, who has lived a highly constrained life since her engagement ended, is ardent for more stringent measures. There is **irony** here also, because in her love affair she was evidently considered by her elders to be acting with extravagant passion in a situation that required the economy of mature common sense.

This theme has obvious relevance to *Persuasion*'s central **ambivalence** in relation to Lady Russell's persuasion of Anne Elliot not to marry. In financial terms, economy (or cautious planning) seems evidently the best approach; but does this also apply in affairs of the heart?

R ISK AND CAUTION

Risk-taking can be profitable, even if it appears in advance to be unwise. Wentworth's rise in status and fortune are testimony to this. Jane Austen makes much in *Persuasion* of the fact that her naval officers have shown daring and courage, and have reaped their rewards. These men are cast in a positive light, so we might well ask whether Anne Elliot might have benefited greatly from ignoring Lady Russell's advocacy of caution.

To have married Frederick Wentworth at the start of his naval career would indeed have been to have taken a risk. But Mrs Croft's happiness with her highly successful husband seems to show that such recklessness can be the best path. On the other hand, Louisa Musgrove's insistence on jumping on the Cobb was an act of wilful impetuosity that nearly resulted in disaster. Caution would have prevented a great deal of distress for all who were present at the accident. In the end, however, the accident did help to secure her marriage to Benwick.

Cautiousness was the **Augustan** way; **Romanticism** championed risk. Which was the most suitable choice for Anne Elliot? That remains for each reader to determine.

S ELFISHNESS AND MUTUALITY

Jane Austen draws clear lines of affinity between the various characters in the novel, and the strongest of these lines are those which link intractably selfish figures, and those which link characters who recognise mutuality or shared interest.

Sir Walter is utterly self-centred, and that characteristic has been transmitted to his daughters Elizabeth and Mary. His heir, William Elliot is also revealed as a man motivated by self-interest, and comparable selfishness underlies the manipulative intrusions of Mrs Clay and her father, Mr Shepherd.

Anne Elliot, on the other hand, has the good fortune to resemble her mother, and her much-vaunted usefulness is a manifestation of her sympathy for other people. Her compassion is evident in her care for little Charles Musgrove, her attention to Louisa, and her friendship with the impoverished Mrs Smith. Above all, her capacity for mutuality is realised in the depth of her love for Wentworth.

He is a man who shares her virtues. Captain Harville turns to him to break the news to Benwick of Fanny Harville's death; and it is Wentworth who volunteers to take news of Louisa's injury to her parents. Later, he will act to assist Mrs Smith where William Elliot failed her. Above all, he really cares for Anne Elliot, as is demonstrated when he secures a lift for her in the Crofts' carriage, saving her from being a single woman in the company of three couples.

The Crofts, and to a lesser extent the elder Musgroves, are models of mutual affection and togetherness. The blisters on Mrs Croft's feet, resulting from the long walks she insists on taking with the Admiral in order to restore his health, are palpable tokens of genuine selflessness.

All is not quite so neatly clear-cut, however. Anne's selflessness is notably compromised when she postpones a visit to Mrs Smith in order to attend a concert, where she might meet Wentworth. Wentworth's love was eclipsed for eight years by a pride which prevented him contacting Anne.

And where are we to locate Lady Russell, when these lines are drawn up? Her love for Anne is asserted regularly, and is a credible continuation of her close friendship with Lady Elliot. Yet she shows repeated insensitivity to Anne's feelings; not least when planning her visit to Bath and, once there, in her apparent fixation with curtains, at that moment when Anne is filled with almost intolerable anguish as her former lover passes by.

PRIDE

Linked to the theme of selfishness and selflessness is that of pride. Pride takes distinct forms in *Persuasion*. There is a negative form, embodied in

Sir Walter, and visible in Lady Russell, which is a kind of snobbishness, or obsession with rank and beauty. There is also a positive form which is manifest in a concern to preserve integrity and dignity.

So, while Sir Walter considers nothing of greater importance than to win the acquaintance of Lady Dalrymple, Anne views his obsequiousness as a travesty of proper pride in the Elliot name. When young William Elliot shows contempt for his family, he is seen by Sir Walter to be offering personal offence, whereas Anne sees his attitude as a violation of family honour. In consequence, when Elliot courts their favour, the rift with Sir Walter is soon healed, but Anne retains a suspicion that this man should not be trusted.

In the broader view, *Persuasion* reflects national pride, following the victory over Napoleon's France. The naval figures in the novel embody that pride, made explicit in its closing paragraph. Jane Austen shared in the sentiment and relied upon it to create certain sympathies amongst contemporary readers.

PERSONAL BIAS AND POINT OF VIEW

Taste is a matter of considerable importance in *Persuasion*. In Bath, some of Wentworth's friends remark that Anne is too delicate for the taste of most men. Wentworth clearly has more discriminating taste. The fact is that no character is free from some form of bias, prejudice or obsession, and that shapes judgement.

All the characters have to make decisions, and in order to do so they have to assume a point of view. Jane Austen shows that this point of view is never neutral, but is always coloured by some aspect of taste. Lady Russell, whose talents as a judge are widely applauded, is very evidently swayed by her respect for rank, and other forms of snobbishness are regularly apparent in her attitudes.

In Chapter 23, Anne and Captain Harville discuss the relative merits of men and women in relation to the virtue of constancy, and the damage resulting from fickleness. Anne concludes by not concluding:

> We never can expect to prove any thing upon such a point. It is a difference of opinion which does not admit of proof. We each begin probably with a little bias towards our own sex, and upon that bias build every circumstance in favour of it which has occurred within our circle. (p. 237)

Ultimately, we, as readers, must also assume a point of view, and it will depend upon our personal bias whether we conclude that Anne was right to follow Lady Russell's advice, or whether we condemn the timidity that led to eight years of unhappiness.

SITUATION

How is Anne Elliot to find a suitable husband? She has no freedom to move through the world on her own, and her social horizons are limited by her father's choice of company. This is invariably not to her liking.

On receiving news of the astonishing alliance between Benwick and Louisa, Anne attributes it to their 'situation', the temporarily shared horizons which have enabled them to discover their affinity. Jane Austen attributes considerable importance to situation in the formation of an individual's fate.

In Chapter 23, during her discussion with Harville, Anne reminds us of the fact that men had almost entire control over the fate of women of her class. Wentworth has entered the world and has changed his situation. Anne, like a heroine in medieval romance, is locked in her tower, as it were, and awaits the arrival of a handsome knight to rescue her from imprisonment.

CONSTANCY

The two preceding themes indicate that Jane Austen recognised a relativism in human affairs. In other words, she saw that understanding and judgement are modified by taste and situation. Such relativism can complicate moral discrimination, but Jane Austen clearly subscribed to a well-defined set of moral values that remained authoritative despite point of view. Honesty and compassion are unequivocally virtues for her, as for most of us.

In matters of the heart, constancy appears to hold a special place for her. Benwick's shift of allegiance from the memory of Fanny Harville to Louisa Musgrove causes waves of surprise to ruffle the social surface in *Persuasion*. Fanny's brother is upset by this development, and Anne has a struggle to excuse it, although she manages to do so. She and Harville have an extended discussion on the topic of constancy, in Chapter 23.

Benwick and Louisa are not dismissed for moral laxity as a result of the love they develop; it is seen as a viable route for them to take. But in contrast, Anne and Wentworth sustain loyal devotion over a long period, and we are left in no doubt that their constancy marks them out as a superior couple.

NARRATIVE TECHNIQUE AND STYLE

NARRATIVE VOICE

As we read *Persuasion*, we are addressed by a narrative voice, which does not belong to any participant in the story, but which does not lay claim to total knowledge of all details, nor assume full understanding of all underlying motives. Rather this voice is marked by confidence that we will share a certain set of values, and will agree with the narrator's view of the world. So, we enter into a process of judging character and interpreting events, which may often be far from straightforward, yet the result will confirm the authority of that shared set of values.

For example, it is evident that the narrator espouses moderation against excess, honesty against duplicity, sensitivity against callousness, intelligence against stupidity, mutuality against selfishness, and it is anticipated that we will do the same. Jane Austen's vocabulary signals clearly where our sympathies should lie in a comparative evaluation of, say, Sir Walter Elliot and Frederick Wentworth. The narrator can safely assume that we will support Anne's position against that of her sister Elizabeth, because there is moral consensus.

SATIRE

Such a consensual understanding of values is a prerequisite for effective **satire**. Deviations from proper behaviour can only be measured if we have a reliable yardstick to gauge what is proper. The twentieth-century satirist, Evelyn Waugh, actually argued that his work could not really be called satire, because in this century we no longer sustain a shared set of values. It is likely, however, that despite many changes in the way we live Jane Austen's readers today will have little trouble in sharing her broad sense of right and wrong, and so will be able to recognise easily the targets of her satirical approach.

AMBIVALENCE

Writing at a time when the taste for **Augustan** values of reason and restraint was being contested by **Romantic** values of passion and spontaneity, Jane Austen seems to have recognised that the consensus on affairs of the heart had been broken. So, the concern of the novel with the relative merits of taking risks and exercising caution, of impetuosity and security, does not lend itself to easy resolution. At the end of *Persuasion*, although we may not trust Lady Russell, we do not feel that we can simply dismiss her interference in Anne's love affair as unjustifiable meddling. The narrative voice allows us to see both sides of the argument, and our sense of right and wrong, in this case, shifts regularly as the novel unfolds. This central issue in *Persuasion* remains **ambivalent**.

FREE INDIRECT STYLE

Although Jane Austen employs a third-person narrative voice, harking back to the example of Henry Fielding, whose work she much admired, there are times when Anne Elliot's perception of events, and response to them, is rendered with a directness that makes them appear far more modern in technique. For example, in Chapter 19, we find this passage:

> No, it was not to be supposed that Lady Russell would perceive him till they were nearly opposite. She looked at her however, from time to time, anxiously; and when the moment approached which must point him out, though not daring to look again (for her own countenance she knew was unfit to be seen), she was yet perfectly conscious of Lady Russell's eyes being turned in exactly the direction for him, of her being in short intently observing him. (p. 188)

The attention here to nuances of perception, and to the fervid operation of Anne's consciousness, anticipates much later developments in **psychological realism**. It might not be too bold to suggest that such sequences in *Persuasion* presage the **stream of consciousness** technique used to great effect a century later by Dorothy Richardson and Virginia Woolf. Jane Austen does not grant us direct access to the workings of

Anne's mind, but her narrative voice is sufficiently flexible and subtle to create that impression on occasion.

Jane Austen was honing her technique to represent fluctuations of feeling. In her first novel, *Sense and Sensibility* she had shown her distaste for the fashionable literature of **sensibility**. She made a further **satirical** attack upon it in her final, incomplete work, *Sanditon*. Jane Austen's distaste was not just for its emotional excess, but also for the crudity of its methods, its floods of tears, and fainting fits. In place of such **melodramatic** effects, she deploys what is now called **free indirect style**. In retrospect we can see what an advance *Persuasion* actually was in the representation of highly charged yet complex interior states. For a fuller discussion of this technique, see Norman Page, *The Language of Jane Austen* (Oxford, 1972).

PARENTHETICAL REMARKS

As may be seen from the passage quoted above, Jane Austen makes particularly effective use of parenthetical remarks. The general effect of these telling comments is to **ironise** the meaning conveyed by the sentences in which they are set. A good example occurs in Chapter 1:

> Be it known then, that Sir Walter, like a good father, (having met with one or two private disappointments in very unreasonable applications) prided himself on remaining single for his dear daughters' sake. (p. 37)

The information contained within the brackets, that Sir Walter had in fact sought to marry women of high status who rejected him, demolishes the validity of the surrounding sentence. Far from being his central concern, his daughters merely provide a means to conceal his embarrassment.

It is worth noting that Virginia Woolf, an appreciative reader of Jane Austen, used the parenthetical remark with great skill to enrich the meaning of her prose, in the early twentieth century.

IRONY

Like the conduct of her heroine, Jane Austen's approach to writing *Persuasion* was undemonstrative, economical, and highly resourceful.

There is no flamboyance in Jane Austen's style, rather it is measured and scrupulously controlled. Yet despite its apparent straightforwardness, appropriate interpretation of events and characters in the novel regularly poses a challenge. This is because of the pervasiveness of Jane Austen's **irony**. This takes numerous forms, but invariably involves a disparity between the meaning that is offered, and a conflicting meaning that is perceived by us, as we read.

So, for example, when Henrietta Musgrove, at the start of Chapter 12, expresses the wish that Dr Shirley should retire and live in Lyme, her ostensible concern is for the curate's health. But we know that the real reason for her view is that she wants Charles Hayter to accede to the Uppercross curacy, in order that she might marry him. We might call this an irony of intention.

She then proceeds to declare:

> I wish Lady Russell lived at Uppercross, and were intimate with Dr Shirley. I have always heard of Lady Russell, as a woman of the greatest influence with every body! I always look upon her as able to persuade a person to any thing! (p. 124)

As she is speaking to Anne Elliot, who has first-hand experience of Lady Russell's powers of persuasion, we may see here another form of irony. If Henrietta's remarks had been addressed to someone who did not know Lady Russell, her words would have assumed a rather different meaning. The speaker is unaware of the weight of significance they will carry for Anne. We might call this an irony of situation.

This is compounded by the fact that Henrietta desires Lady Russell to engage in an act of persuasion that will assist her marriage to Hayter, while Anne is confronted with the memory of that persuasion which ended her own engagement.

For an in-depth discussion of Jane Austen's irony, see Marvin Mudrick, *Jane Austen: Irony as Defense and Discovery* (Princeton, 1952).

THEATRICAL ELEMENTS

As well as being adept in rendering subtleties of perception, thought, and feeling, Jane Austen was a very skilful utiliser of dramatic techniques. The Austen family were keen on theatre, and their barn at Steventon was drawn into service for the performance of plays, which they wrote and enacted themselves. It is arguable that the legacy of these family theatricals may be detected in the mature novelist's accomplished use of dialogue to further the action, and to furnish insight into character, or in dramatic set-pieces, such as Louisa's accident on the Cobb.

Note the care with which Jane Austen locates figures within the space of a room, and the expert way in which she handles their movement towards or away from one another, their arrival and departure. In *Persuasion* there are many instances which might be cited.

A good example occurs in Chapter 9, when Anne is attending to her injured nephew Charles. Captain Wentworth stands by a window; Charles Hayter sits reading next to a table. The spatial separation of the characters reflects the tensions between them, which preclude easy conversation. Little Walter Musgrove enters and, ignoring Hayter's efforts to draw him to himself, the infant clings to Anne and hinders her care of young Charles. Wentworth silently strides across the room to seize the child, freeing Anne from his grasp. The entire scene is a triumph of expressive choreography.

Jane Austen's liking for theatrical convention may also be detected in her less sophisticated recourse to the contrivance of coincidence. The fortuitous letting of Kellynch-hall to Wentworth's brother-in-law, or the chance encounter with William Elliot in Lyme seem improbable, but the inclusion of such elements heightens dramatic tension and facilitates rapid development of the plot.

PART FOUR

TEXTUAL ANALYSIS

TEXT 1 (PAGES 42–4)

They must retrench; that did not admit of a doubt. But she was very anxious to have it done with the least possible pain to him and Elizabeth. She drew up plans of economy, she made exact calculations, and she did, what nobody else thought of doing, she consulted Anne, who never seemed considered by the others as having any interest in the question. She consulted, and in a degree was influenced by her, in marking out the scheme of retrenchment, which was at last submitted to Sir Walter. Every emendation of Anne's had been on the side of honesty against importance. She wanted more vigorous measures, a more complete reformation, a quicker release from debt, a much higher tone of indifference for every thing but justice and equity.

'If we can persuade your father to all this,' said Lady Russell, looking over her paper, 'much may be done. If he will adopt these regulations, in seven years he will be clear; and I hope we may be able to convince him and Elizabeth, that Kellynch-hall has a respectability in itself, which cannot be affected by these reductions; and that the true dignity of Sir Walter Elliot will be very far from lessened in the eyes of sensible people, by his acting like a man of principle. What will he be doing, in fact, but what very many of our first families have done – or ought to do? – There will be nothing singular in his case; and it is singularity which often makes the worst part of our suffering, as it always does of our conduct. I have great hope of our prevailing. We must be serious and decided – for, after all, the person who has contracted debts must pay them; and though a great deal is due to the feelings of the gentleman, and the head of a house, like your father, there is still more due to the character of an honest man.'

This was the principle on which Anne wanted her father to be proceeding, his friends to be urging him. She considered it as an act of indispensable duty to clear away the claims of creditors, with all the expedition which the most comprehensive retrenchments could secure, and saw no dignity in any thing short of it. She wanted it to be prescribed, and felt as a duty. She rated Lady Russell's influence highly, and as to the severe degree of self-denial, which her own conscience prompted, she believed there might be little more difficulty in persuading them to a complete, than to half a reformation. Her knowledge of her father and Elizabeth, inclined her to think that the sacrifice of one pair of horses would be hardly less painful than of both, and so on, through the whole list of Lady Russell's too gentle reductions.

How Anne's more rigid requisitions might have been taken, is of little consequence. Lady Russell's had no success at all – could not be put up with – were not to be borne. 'What! Every comfort of life knocked off! Journeys, London, servants, horses, table, – contractions and restrictions every where. To live no longer with the decencies even of a private gentleman! No, he would sooner quit Kellynch-hall at once, than remain in it on such disgraceful terms.'

'She' is Lady Russell, who has been described, immediately before this passage, as 'a benevolent, charitable, good woman', who is 'capable of strong attachments'. She is 'most correct in her conduct, strict in her notions of decorum, and with manners that were held as a standard of good breeding' (p. 42). The description is clearly intended to endorse the authority of this cultivated woman, and her reputation as an excellent judge seems entirely credible in the light of such testimony.

But a warning note has been sounded: we learn that while she is 'generally speaking, rational and consistent', Lady Russell has 'prejudices on the side of ancestry'. Her respect for rank blinkers her to the faults of those who possess it. This blind spot appears to align her, in this crucial respect, with Sir Walter Elliot, whose foolishness has been made manifest in the opening chapter. Indeed, she is prepared to display 'a great deal of compassion and consideration' towards Sir Walter. The vocabulary of positive values and admirable qualities is reserved throughout for Anne Elliot and Frederick Wentworth. The extension of compassion to the spendthrift baronet seems to be a misapplication of that valuable sentiment. We may feel inclined to mistrust Lady Russell's judgement, and to watch for further evidence that she is in effect abusing the confidence placed in her.

This passage from Chapter 2 opens with an example of **free indirect style**. The voice belongs to the narrator, but we recognise that the words, 'They must retrench; that did not admit of a doubt', report faithfully a direct utterance made by Lady Russell. Note that she is keen to avoid causing 'pain' to Sir Walter and Elizabeth in this matter. There is **irony** here; the word 'pain' is used to describe Anne's emotional turmoil following the termination of her engagement to Wentworth. Of course, that also followed Lady Russell's persuasive intervention, and her advice then was equally bound to matters of economy. Wentworth's future was by no means financially assured. There may also be a suggestion that the young couple's passionate love was an indulgence, which had to be reined in by such 'plans of economy' and 'exact calculations' as Lady Russell is seen executing in this case.

Once we have recognised this irony, a crucial **ambivalence** informs our perception of this supposedly wise and kindly woman. She has sufficient perspicacity to consult Anne who, after all, is immediately affected by any changes at Kellynch-hall. Jane Austen does not allow the general neglect of Anne to be taken as an indication of her own unworthiness; rather it reflects the obtuseness of the other members of the Elliot family. Lady Russell is certainly not obtuse in this respect.

On the other hand, we can see how her measured and methodical approach to Sir Walter's problems would have been extended eight years earlier to Anne's engagement, and we are aware of the devitalising effect it had upon the nineteen-year-old, whose looks have deteriorated as a consequence. Was Lady Russell's calculated wisdom sufficiently responsive to the emotional life of her young friend? That is a key question which is raised by a succession of episodes throughout the novel. It is essential to Jane Austen's thematic concern with the relative merits of risk and caution in the conduct of life (see Theme on Risk and Caution).

Prudent planning is unquestionably a necessary corrective to the extravagance that characterises Sir Walter's thoughtless and recklessly selfish conduct. Anne goes further than her friend in proposing stringent measures. This might be seen as a reflection of her own constrained horizons, and of a rather prudish taste for modest living which developed following her disappointment in love. But the narrator ensures that a positive slant is put upon her rigour: 'Every emendation of Anne's had been on the side of honesty against importance'. It is assumed that 'honesty' will be commonly held to be an admirable virtue. To consolidate this consensual moral evaluation of Anne, she is said to be driven by dedication to 'justice and equity'. The vocabulary speaks the narrator's approval of this virtuous young woman, and anticipates our agreement (see Narrative Technique and Style on Narrative Voice).

There is a shift to direct speech, as Lady Russell predicts that a successful act of persuasion will amend Sir Walter's fortunes in the space of seven years. We may detect further **irony** here, as it is now eight years since she intervened to direct Anne's course of life, and it becomes increasingly evident that she has not yet recovered from the effect of that intervention.

Still, Lady Russell's recognition of the 'respectability' that inheres in Kellynch-hall, and of the 'dignity' which resides in the baronetcy is shared by Anne, even though she is acutely aware of her father's habitual lapses from the dignity proper to his rank. Anne's pride in her family's position, if not in their actual behaviour, is presented as one of the traits that distinguish her superiority. A recurrent thematic concern of *Persuasion* is the dual nature of pride, a virtue in some contexts and a distinct failing in others (see Theme on Pride). There is a snobbish form of pride in Lady Russell's inability to see that Sir Walter would not appear 'a man of principle' in the eyes of 'sensible' people.

Lady Russell draws a general moral from Sir Walter's case; his retrenchment will conform to what many leading families have done, or should do: 'There will be nothing singular in his case; and it is singularity which often makes the worst part of our suffering, as it always does of our conduct'. The distaste for singularity is very much in keeping with the **Augustan** taste which would have prevailed during Lady Russell's formative years. Dr Johnson, whom Jane Austen greatly admired, abhorred any manifestation of eccentricity or wilful abnormality.

The **Romantic** taste of the early nineteenth century, on the other hand, sought out the singular, the abnormal, and the strange. Romantic essayists, such as Thomas De Quincey and William Hazlitt, dwelt with fascination on peculiarities. Hazlitt's evaluation of the character of the late William Pitt, published in 1806, began with the assertion that it was 'one of the most singular that ever existed' (see Literary Background).

Anne Elliot shares Lady Russell's inclination to project a general case from a particular instance. Perhaps we should recognise this as one indication of the older woman's influence upon her. But if she has the capacity for Augustan sagacity, Anne is also a reader of Lord Byron, and at crucial moments in the novel (such as her cancellation of an appointment to meet with Mrs Smith) she subordinates social obligations to the dictates of her passion for Wentworth. Anne's life straddles a notable shift in popular taste. Upon this fact, Jane Austen builds the essential **ambivalence** of the novel (see Narrative Technique and Style on Ambivalence).

The narration returns to the **free indirect style**, and initially grants us privileged access to the workings of Anne's mind. 'This was the principle on which Anne wanted her father to be proceeding, his friends to be urging him', does not appear to reflect an actual utterance, but to disclose unspoken approval for Lady Russell's proposals. Her emphasis on 'duty' and 'dignity' in the sentences that follow, marks an affinity with the older woman's values. But just as Lady Russell's point of view is susceptible to bias based on her respect for status, so we may suspect that Anne's advocacy of stringency reflects a life of emotional sacrifice and self-denial, following the ending of her love affair. This conforms to *Persuasion*'s thematic concern with the way that points of view which enable judgement are shaped by differing degrees of personal obsession (see Theme on Personal Bias and Point of View).

The concluding sentence of the paragraph, which shows how well Anne understands her father and elder sister, could conceivably reflect an actual utterance. She may be envisaged telling her friend that 'the sacrifice of one pair of horses would be hardly less painful than of both'. The narration is moving towards the report of Sir Walter's response, which has little to do with rational introspection, and bears all the hallmarks of a **melodramatic** emotional outburst.

The sentence 'Lady Russell's [requisitions] had no success at all – could not be put up with – were not to be borne', shifts from third-person commentary to reported speech. The narrative voice is conveying Lady Russell's voice (filled with dismay), conveying Sir Walter's response (filled with haughty dismissiveness). Quotation marks then introduce a series of ejaculations that at first appear to proceed from Sir Walter directly. The concluding declaration, however, refers to Sir Walter as 'he', and it becomes evident that the voice we are encountering within the quotation marks belongs to Lady Russell rather than the baronet. She appears to be reporting his response in a distilled form, leaving us in no doubt that she feels frustrated by him to the point of outrage.

Although she continues to revere rank, it is clear later in the novel that Lady Russell and the stubborn baronet are rather less friendly than we were initially led to believe. This is necessary if we are not to feel her purported wisdom to be extensively compromised by that friendship. Her devotion to Anne is substantially to her favour, and enables us to continue to view her as in essential ways a sympathetic character. Without that element of sympathy, the central **ambivalence** of the novel would be jeopardised.

This passage is followed by a characteristically opportunistic act by Mr Shepherd. The lawyer turns Sir Walter's exclamation that he would sooner quit Kellynch-hall than undergo such economies into a proposal, which he concertedly endorses and subsequently enforces. In contrast to the naval officers, who offer such a positive view of professional men in Georgian England, this lawyer is portrayed as a sinister figure, manipulating circumstances to his own financial advantage. Although he does not appear throughout most of the book, his daughter Mrs Clay proves a disarming presence in the Elliot household. To what extent should we see Shepherd's influence at work, even in his absence? Remember that it was the lawyer who arranged for Admiral Croft to rent Kellynch-hall, and without that circumstance there would have been no story of reconciliation between Anne and Wentworth.

TEXT 2   (PAGES 177–9)

In her own room she tried to comprehend it. Well might Charles wonder how Captain Wentworth would feel! Perhaps he had quitted the field, had given Louisa up, had ceased to love, had found he did not love her. She could not endure the idea of treachery or levity, or any thing akin to ill-usage between him and his friend. She could not endure that such a friendship as theirs should be severed unfairly.

Captain Benwick and Louisa Musgrove! The high-spirited, joyous, talking Louisa Musgrove, and the dejected, thinking, feeling, reading Captain Benwick, seemed each of them every thing that would not suit the other. Their minds most dissimilar! Where could have been the attraction? The answer soon presented itself. It had been in situation. They had been thrown together several weeks; they had been living in the same small family party; since Henrietta's coming away, they must have been depending almost entirely on each other, and Louisa, just recovering from illness, had been in an interesting state, and Captain Benwick was not inconsolable. That was a point which Anne had not been able to avoid suspecting before; and instead of drawing the same conclusion as Mary, from the present course of events, they served only to confirm the idea of his having felt some dawning of tenderness toward herself. She did not mean, however, to derive much more from it to gratify her vanity, than Mary might have allowed. She was persuaded that any tolerably pleasing young woman who had listened and seemed to feel for him, would have received the same compliment. He had an affectionate heart. He must love somebody.

She saw no reason against their being happy. Louisa had fine naval fervour to begin with, and they would soon grow more alike. He would gain cheerfulness, and she would learn to be an enthusiast for Scott and Lord Byron; nay, that was probably learnt already; of course they had fallen in love over poetry. The idea of Louisa Musgrove turned into a person of literary taste, and sentimental reflection, was amusing, but she had no doubt of its being so. The day at Lyme, the fall from the Cobb, might influence her health, her nerves, her courage, her character to the end of her life, as thoroughly as it appeared to have influenced her fate.

The conclusion of the whole was, that if the woman who had been sensible of Captain Wentworth's merits could be allowed to prefer another man, there was nothing in the engagement to excite lasting wonder; and if Captain Wentworth lost no friend by it, certainly nothing to be regretted. No, it was not regret which made Anne's heart beat in spite of herself, and brought the colour into her cheeks when she thought of Captain Wentworth unshackled and free. She had some feelings which she was ashamed to investigate. They were too much like joy, senseless joy!

She longed to see the Crofts, but when the meeting took place, it was evident that no rumour of the news had yet reached them. The visit of ceremony was paid and returned, and Louisa Musgrove was mentioned, and Captain Benwick too, without even half a smile.

The Crofts had placed themselves in lodgings in Gay-street, perfectly to Sir Walter's satisfaction. He was not at all ashamed of the acquaintance, and did, in fact, think and talk a great deal more about the Admiral, than the Admiral ever thought or talked about him.

This passage in Chapter 18 is one of the rare moments in the novel when we see Anne alone. Buildings and rooms generally have social significance in *Persuasion*; they indicate status, and furnish settings for public events and family gatherings. Anne's own room is a private space, and provides an appropriate context for consideration of issues of intimate significance to her.

The third-person narration shifts into **free indirect style** in order to grant us access to Anne's thoughts concerning Wentworth's disappearance from Lyme, and the announcement of Benwick's engagement to Louisa Musgrove. Her actual thought processes are mediated by the narrative voice, so although we are placed, effectively, inside her head, critical detachment is preserved through the third-person formula, 'She could not endure ...'. Although we may feel strong sympathy for Anne, we remain spectators to her actions and responses (see Narrative Technique and Style).

Anne conceives that Wentworth might have 'quitted the field'. The **metaphor** invokes **chivalric romance**, casting him as a knight withdrawing from a contest to win the heart of a lady. The chivalric code of conduct is an **anachronism**, but it elucidates the view Anne holds of her former lover. Immediately before this passage, Sir Walter refers to 'several odd-looking men walking about here, who, I am told, are sailors'. In contrast to his absurd obsession with appearance, Anne dwells on the code of honour to which naval officers adhere. It binds Wentworth to Benwick, and she hopes that no violation of honour has occurred in the winning of Louisa. Anne's recognition of standards for moral guidance is entirely alien to her father, whose motivation is always craven self-interest.

Notice how, within the context of free indirect style, Anne's astonishment at the news is rendered with intensity through the strategic use of an exclamation mark: 'Captain Benwick and Louisa Musgrove!'. The punctuation mark conveys to us the complex mix of confusion, excitement, and disbelief that comprises Anne's response. That response is then elaborated through a telling alignment of adjectives: 'high-spirited, joyous, talking' (Louisa); 'dejected, thinking, feeling, reading' (Benwick). In a novel where such contrast often provides moral guidance for readers, this adjectival differentiation is just an assertion of difference. If we sense that Anne has more in common with the sensitive and literary-minded Benwick, 'dejected' yet defies a more positive reading than 'joyous'.

The two are held in balance, and this may be seen to anticipate the **ambivalence** which remains unresolved at the end of the novel: the dilemma of risk-taking versus exercising caution. These dissimilar characters are drawn together, Anne observes, as a result of 'situation'. Their proximity generated mutual attraction. The suggestion is that by adapting principle to context a practicable course may be followed between recklessness and reserve (see Themes).

But Anne's musings are not as detached as this discussion might suggest. She is, of course, intimately involved in the unfolding of these developments. It is to her satisfaction that she recognises that Benwick probably did develop a romantic attachment to her during their conversations at Lyme. This confirms to her that, at twenty-seven and with her looks diminished, she does still hold attraction for men, and that has evident implications for her future relationship to one man in particular.

It is consistent with Jane Austen's characterisation of Anne elsewhere that she is seen here to derive a typical lesson from a particular case. Benwick is not merely a case of aberrant singularity; rather, 'He had an affectionate heart. He must love somebody'. It seems likely that she considers herself a comparable type, although we should remember that she has turned down Charles Musgrove's proposal of marriage, and has demonstrated herself to be a model of constancy, despite being the instrument of her own fate in deciding to reject Wentworth (see Theme on Constancy). If she does align herself with Benwick, it signals her passionate longing, but in this she contrasts with the practical action Benwick has taken in order to dispel his grief. It is important to note that Anne was not able, as a woman of her class, to take the lead as Benwick has; her fate was to await an appropriate proposal.

Certainly, Anne shares Benwick's enthusiasm for poetry, and she concludes that it was Scott and Byron who provided the meeting point for Louisa and Benwick's disparate temperaments. To grant poetry such a signal role, with the anticipation that from that conjunction the lovers will grow increasingly to recognise their common interests and attributes, is a bold step for Jane Austen. Anne seems to be assigning art a special status on account of its blending of passion and intellect.

Perhaps a more telling insight into Anne's character arises from her belief that Louisa's fall on the Cobb 'might influence her health, her nerves, her courage, her character to the end of her life, as thoroughly as it appeared to have influenced her fate'. There can be little doubt that a parallel is being assumed here between Louisa's physical injury, and the trauma Anne endured when she sacrificed her love for Wentworth.

Circumstances may modify character; Anne derives this lesson from her own experience. But there are continuities in character also, and it is the persistence of her numerous virtues which will eventually reawaken Wentworth's love for her, to the point where it dominates his behaviour. Continuity in Louisa is recognised, with **irony**, in Anne's conclusion that 'if the woman who had been sensible of Captain Wentworth's merits could be allowed to prefer another man, there was nothing in the engagement to excite lasting wonder'.

Anne's judgement echoes Lady Russell's unspoken delight, in Chapter 13, that Wentworth, who had once valued Anne Elliot, now admired a mere Louisa Musgrove. The echo signals the alignment of the older and younger woman in their tendency to make such discriminations. Both also are motivated in these particular verdicts by unmistakable self-interest. In Anne's case this is made particularly clear with the declaration that her feelings 'were too much like joy, senseless joy!'.

Anne's desire to speak with the Crofts, who are visiting Bath, is motivated basically by her keenness to garner further insight into Wentworth's position. It is noteworthy that in the course of their discussion, she ventured to mention Louisa and Benwick, and took on board the Crofts' apparent ignorance of developments. There is no sign that Mrs Croft's brother was openly considered, and that is indicative of the constraints placed upon women of Anne's class in Jane Austen's day. As mentioned above, it would have been quite improper for her to have made any enquiry which might have been perceived as driven by amorous interest. It may also be taken as a token of Anne's agitated sensitivity that no reference to Wentworth is made in the report of her encounter with the Crofts.

In contrast to his daughter's inner turbulence, to which he is perfectly oblivious, Sir Walter pursues his shallow interest in the display of social status. He is able to approve of the lodgings taken by the Crofts, which he adjudges sufficiently respectable to permit his acquaintance with them. We have moved rapidly away from the interior of Anne's private room.

The concluding touch is an incisive contrast between the superficial and facile baronet, and the honest, commonsensical Admiral. The folly of this effete aristocrat is highlighted through the relative indifference towards him displayed by the worldly professional man.

TEXT 3   (PAGES 235–7)

'Look here,' said he, unfolding a parcel in his hand, and displaying a small miniature painting, 'do you know who that is?'

'Certainly, Captain Benwick.'

'Yes, and you may guess who it is for. But (in a deep tone) it was not done for her. Miss Elliot, do you remember our walking together at Lyme, and grieving for him? I little thought then – but no matter. This was drawn at the Cape. He met with a clever young German artist at the Cape, and in compliance with a promise to my poor sister, sat to him, and was bringing it home for her. And I have now the charge of getting it properly set for another! It was a commission to me! But who else was there to employ? I hope I can allow for him. I am not sorry, indeed, to make it over to another. He undertakes it – (looking towards Captain Wentworth) he is writing about it now.' And with a quivering lip he wound up the whole by adding, 'Poor Fanny! she would not have forgotten him so soon!'

'No,' replied Anne, in a low feeling voice. 'That I can easily believe.'

'It was not in her nature. She doated on him.'

'It would not be in the nature of any woman who truly loved.'

Captain Harville smiled, as much as to say, 'Do you claim that for your sex?' and she answered the question, smiling also, 'Yes. We certainly do not forget you, so soon as you forget us. It is, perhaps, our fate rather than our merit. We cannot help ourselves. We live at home, quiet, confined, and our feelings prey upon us. You are forced on exertion. You have always a profession, pursuits, business of some sort or other, to take you back into the world immediately, and continual occupation and change soon weaken impressions.'

'Granting your assertion that the world does all this so soon for men, (which, however, I do not think I shall grant) it does not apply to Benwick. He has not been forced upon any exertion. The peace turned him on shore at the very moment, and he has been living with us, in our little family-circle, ever since.'

'True,' said Anne, 'very true; I did not recollect; but what shall we say now, Captain Harville? If the change be not from outward circumstances, it must be from within; it must be nature, man's nature, which has done the business for Captain Benwick.'

'No, no, it is not man's nature. I will not allow it to be more man's nature than woman's to be inconstant and forget those they do love, or have loved. I believe the reverse. I believe in a true analogy between our bodily frames and our mental; and that as our bodies are the strongest, so are our feelings; capable of bearing most rough usage, and riding out the heaviest weather.'

'Your feelings may be the strongest,' replied Anne, 'but the same spirit of analogy will authorise me to assert that ours are the most tender. Man is more robust than woman, but he is not longer-lived; which exactly explains my view of the nature of their attachments. Nay, it would be too hard upon you, if it were otherwise. You have difficulties, and privations, and dangers enough to struggle with. You are always labouring and toiling, exposed to every risk and hardship. Your home, country, friends, all quitted. Neither time, nor health, nor life, to be called your own. It would be too hard indeed' (with a faltering voice) 'if woman's feelings were to be added to all this.'

This passage from Chapter 23 is a notable example of Jane Austen's craft in staging scenes, of her skilful arrangement of figures in space to create dramatic effects, charged with meaning (see Narrative Technique and Style on Theatrical Elements). Anne has joined Captain Harville by a window. Wentworth writes a letter at a table nearby. The conversation and the letter-writing are independent activities, as is evident from the space between them. But Wentworth is close enough to overhear what is said. Anne is aware of this, and it conditions her utterances, with vital consequences in the ensuing action, towards the conclusion of the novel.

The effects of this arrangement are heightened by the fact that Mrs Croft and Mrs Musgrove converse at the other end of the room. It is clear that Anne has heard some of their discussion concerning the need to ensure financial security in marriage, and has felt the relevance of these remarks to her own situation. Preoccupied by the issues raised, the conversation becomes 'a buzz of words in her ear, her mind was in confusion'. Harville, prior to his move to the window 'had in truth been hearing none of it'; he has been otherwise preoccupied.

Now he addresses Anne directly, showing her a miniature portrait of Benwick, intended now for Louisa, but executed for Harville's sister, Fanny. Note the parenthetical, '(in a deep tone)', which operates here like a stage direction, indicating appropriate delivery to an actor. The 'deep tone' discloses depth of feeling; Harville is genuinely upset by what he perceives as his friend's inconstancy to his sister's memory. The value of constancy is one of the thematic concerns of *Persuasion* (see Theme on Constancy).

Wentworth is portrayed as a steady and constant friend, who can be relied upon to act to assist a friend in distress. Benwick's request that Harville should have the painting framed for him seems remarkably insensitive. Wentworth is fortunately at hand to undertake the commission. We may perhaps find some excuse for Benwick in his current preoccupation with Louisa, but it is evident that he and Wentworth are being offered for our comparative evaluation, and we have to conclude that Benwick has found an appropriate partner, while Wentworth is worthy of Anne Elliot.

As we have seen in Text 2, the apparent inconstancy of Benwick has challenged Anne's sense of propriety, although she has come to terms with her uneasiness by categorising him as a type, as a man who needed to be loved. As noted above, Benwick has the great advantage, as a man in a society oriented towards men, of being able to escape his grief through proposal of marriage to another woman. Anne, as a woman of her class, has to endure a passive role. Harville is here suggesting that it is improper for a man to become engaged so quickly after such a loss. Whatever the arguments for and against this ethical view, it is surely telling that the conversation with Anne moves swiftly to discuss the disadvantages suffered by women on account of the social restrictions that prevailed in patriarchal Georgian society.

Anne's proclivity to draw large conclusions from localised instances makes her a credible participant in the more generalised phase of this conversation, allowing Jane Austen to introduce some pungent social criticism, which has won the support of later feminist readers (see Contemporary Approaches: Feminist). Anne's experience of life is very limited, as was Jane Austen's. But she shares with the author the capacity to exercise reason in the service of moral insight. The conditions delimiting the scope of her existence are in fact the main topic for discussion.

After asserting that women are more inclined to constancy in love than men, (an observation extrapolated from her own feelings, and delivered in the awareness that her former lover sits nearby), she addresses the ways in which 'situation' conditions attitudes. 'Situation' was a further explanation she discerned for Benwick's rapid attachment to Louisa, the suggestion being that when individuals share a common set of horizons to their experience they discover unexpected forms of allegiance (see Theme on Situation).

Anne herself found common horizons with Benwick in their appreciation of literature. But literature offers, ultimately, a vicarious mode of existence, and she now makes a plea for the case of women:

> We live at home, quiet, confined, and our feelings prey upon us. You are forced on exertion. You have always a profession, pursuits, business of some sort or other, to take you back into the world immediately, and continual occupation and change soon weaken impressions.

The broad psychological point being made here is that activity weakens the grip of a particular attachment. Keeping busy is a good way to overcome grief. The socially critical point is that women are confined in such a way that they know few distractions. So, love is liable to remain constant (to put a positive slant upon the situation), or may remain a painful obsession (to view it in a negative light).

A Marxist critic would necessarily point out that Anne speaks here only for women of the upper classes. Servants and other working women would have little leisure to dwell on lost love. Does that mean that they are less likely to prove constant? Harville sees Anne's claim as being made on behalf of her 'sex'; we should recognise that it is made also for her class. The Marxist critic might also observe that working-class men would generally have known far less mobility, and far more routine than the professional men of business and commerce of whom Anne speaks (see Contemporary Approaches: Historicist).

Jane Austen tended to offer psychological and moral insights as if they held universal application, when in fact they had a clear class dimension that limited their veracity. This does not necessarily diminish her accomplishment as a writer, but it does require that we read with critical alertness. The very fact that certain kinds of people are excluded from her consideration may grant us insight into the conditions of their social existence. So, a post-colonial critic may develop an illuminating consideration of the lives of colonised people in the West Indies, based on the fact that although Jane Austen refers to wealth generated in those colonies, she does not show any awareness of the conditions of existence experienced by those whose labour produced that wealth (see Contemporary Approaches: Post-Colonial).

Here Jane Austen seems to be using Anne to formulate a feminist position. She was actually a deeply conservative woman, and it is arguable that her objections to patriarchy manifest a personal grievance, rather than forming a genuinely political analysis of the kind found in Mary Wollstonecraft's *Vindication of the Rights of Woman* (1792). It is evident that Jane Austen was acutely conscious, from her own family, of the disparities of education and experience between men and women of her class. Two of her brothers were admirals, and the presence of two nautical men in this scene heightens the sense that Anne's existence is narrowly cloistered.

Mention of 'the peace' recalls the recent conclusion of the war against Napoleon. Anne is enjoying a contest of wits with Harville, but it would have been inconceivable to her, as to Jane Austen, that women could participate, as men had, in the defence of their country. Jane Austen, and most of her contemporary readers would have considered men's participation gallant and proper. In comparison to the urgency of effective conduct during wartime, the case against men in affairs of the heart seems of markedly less importance. Jane Austen, who in a letter referred to the scope of her fictional world as a 'little bit (two Inches wide) of Ivory' would surely have accepted that evaluation.

Nonetheless, Anne continues the debate by tracing inconstancy to man's nature. Harville rebuffs her with the assertion that 'as our bodies are the strongest, so are our feelings'. His strategy of analogy is countered by Anne, who is evidently not prepared to concede the faculty of logic to masculine intelligence alone: 'Man is more robust than woman, but he is not longer-lived; which exactly explains my view of the nature of their attachments'.

The passage ends with another telling parenthetical comment. Anne concludes her address '(with a faltering voice)'. Again, we can see how the scene has been conceived as a performed dialogue. Anne seems to be stridently engaged in friendly argument with Harville, but the brackets contain a clear indication that she is acutely conscious of Wentworth's presence. The discussion has an obvious bearing on their shared situation, and it is evident that Anne is speaking, if indirectly, to the man she still loves. His understanding of that is confirmed immediately afterwards when he drop his pen. We are told that Anne felt that he had not heard her argument, but that is surely disingenuous. In any case, the letter that she receives soon afterwards is proof that her message was received and understood: Wentworth in turn confirms the constancy of his love.

PART FIVE

BACKGROUND

JANE AUSTEN

Jane Austen was born in Steventon, Hampshire, on 16 December 1775. Her father George Austen was a clergyman, who had married Cassandra Leigh, in Bath, in 1764. The couple had eight children, and Jane was the seventh. Her sister Cassandra had been born two years earlier. The other children were boys.

The Reverend Austen was Rector of Steventon, and his family was financially secure and close-knit. Much of what we know about Jane Austen's life has been learned from correspondence between them. The Austens belonged to the 'gentry', the social class below the nobility. In fact, Jane's brother Edward was adopted by a wealthy but childless aristocrat, and in time inherited his large estate. It is indicative of the Austens' perceived status that the boy was considered suitable for such a responsibility. The gentry forms the focus for most of Jane Austen's fiction. Family relationships held distinctly positive value for her, and the portrayal of the Elliots in *Persuasion* should be read with this in mind.

Jane's formal education was limited. In 1782, she and Cassandra Austen were sent away to school in Oxford. The school moved to Southampton, and the girls were then withdrawn, following an outbreak of illness. The Austen sisters attended another school in Reading for a while, before returning home. Jane Austen then remained with her family for most of the rest of her life. Anne Elliot's sense of the cloistered lives of women is firmly based in the author's own experience.

George Austen was a highly educated man, with an extensive knowledge of classical literature. He acted as private tutor to a number of wealthy local children. At home, Jane drew benefit from that knowledge and experience, and had access to her father's substantial library. She read French well, and had some knowledge of Italian. Like other women of her class, she played piano well, could sing and dance, and was skilled in needlecraft.

Jane Austen was fortunate in having an educated and enlightened father, but the society in which she grew up nonetheless disadvantaged women in a number of important areas. Their basic education was considerably more restrictive, and they were not able to attend university in order to develop their education. They lacked rights of inheritance which were common to men, and had no real means to achieve financial independence. Marriage therefore had a particularly weighty significance in their lives, and Lady Russell's cautious sense of the need for financial security should be viewed in this light. Anne cannot take matters into her own hands; she has to wait for a proposal from Wentworth. The Kellynch estate is to be left to a male relative, despite the fact that Sir Walter has three daughters.

In 1801, George Austen retired, and took his wife and daughters to live in Bath. It is reported that Jane fainted when she was told of the move. Her distaste for upheaval was compounded by her suffering from Addison's Disease, an illness affecting the kidneys, which eventually took her life. The lodgings the Austens found in the city were similar to those taken by the Elliots. Anne's response to the card-playing party-goers of Bath, with their self-conscious concern for appearance is a fair reflection of Jane Austen's own perception of the place and its inhabitants, although its reputation as the centre of fashionable society had by then passed to Brighton. It was while resident at Bath that Jane Austen visited Lyme Regis, in Dorset.

Like Anne Elliot, Jane Austen knew no financial independence. Her father died in 1805, leaving his wife and two daughters a paltry annual sum. The women were supported with generous assistance from the rector's sons. Charles and Frank Austen were naval officers, who eventually became admirals; other brothers had joined the army and entered the church. Sailors, soldiers, and clergymen are familiar figures in her fiction, as in her life. The navy is especially prominent in *Persuasion*, set as it is in the aftermath of the Napoleonic wars.

In 1809, Jane and Cassandra moved with their mother to a cottage at Chawton, adjacent to Edward Austen's estate. Jane remained there, writing novels, until 1817, when she moved to Winchester, where necessary medical assistance was more readily available. In July of that year, at the age of 42, she died, in the arms of her sister, Cassandra. She was buried in Winchester Cathedral. In 1818, a volume was published posthumously. It contained two novels: *Northanger Abbey* and *Persuasion*.

There have been numerous biographies of Jane Austen. Elizabeth Jenkins's *Jane Austen, a Biography* (1938; revised 1948) was for many years the standard volume. Subsequent books have offered some new information, and re-evaluation of older assessments. Particularly worthy of note are: Park Honan, *Jane Austen: Her Life* (London, 1987); John Halperin, *The Life of Jane Austen* (Brighton, 1984); David Nokes, *Jane Austen* (London, 1997). An attractive, illustrated introduction is offered by Marghanita Laski's *Jane Austen* (London, 1975).

HER OTHER WORKS

Jane Austen started writing when she was a child. Her first published novel was *Sense and Sensibility* (1811), which she had completed in 1795, when only twenty years old. Initially, she wrote it in the form of a series of letters, but the final version rejected this **epistolary** mode, learnt from Samuel Richardson, and despite her declared taste for Richardson she did not return to that technique for any of her completed novels. Instead, she worked, with increasing sophistication, with third-person narration.

Jane Austen was not a professional writer; it was only in the last years of her life that she acquired some income from her novels, which she continued to view very much as a leisure pursuit. Nonetheless, her reputation grew to the extent that she heard her work was admired by the Prince Regent (later George IV), and when *Emma* was published, in 1816, it was respectfully dedicated to him.

Although she wrote of family matters, love affairs, and social manners, Jane Austen was an accomplished **satirist**, and the comic elements in her novels should not be overlooked. The tone of her humour changed between the early novels, written while she lived at Steventon, and the later work, completed at Chawton. The first group, comprising *Pride and Prejudice* (1796; published 1813), *Sense and Sensibility* (published 1811), and *Northanger Abbey* (1798; published 1818) are noticeably lighter in tone. *Mansfield Park* (1814), *Emma* (1816) and *Persuasion* (1818) are altogether less high-spirited, more alert to sadness and cruelty encountered in life.

The publication of *Northanger Abbey* and *Persuasion* in one posthumous volume provided a piquant contrast. The earlier novel includes a lively **parody** of the **Gothic** mode, popularised by writers such as Ann Radcliffe. *Persuasion* accommodates more graciously facets of **Romantic** literary taste, incorporating them into its enquiry into relationships between taste and judgement.

HISTORICAL BACKGROUND

THE WAR AGAINST NAPOLEON

The immediately apparent historical background to *Persuasion* is provided through references to the recently fought Napoleonic wars. Jane Austen knew, from the experiences of her own family, the anxiety that was felt by relatives of those at risk in the conflict. She was also keenly aware of the enhancement of personal prospects which could ensue from participation. It was possible to be promoted within the service, but there was also substantial prize-money to be gained from capture of enemy vessels. Captain Wentworth is a beneficiary of the wars, but the conclusion of the novel sounds a note of concern about the price which might be paid for such advancement.

Inevitably, in the aftermath of Napoleon's defeat at Waterloo, there was a surge of national pride, with especial recognition for the valour displayed by the British navy, in triumphs such as the Battle of Trafalgar. Jane Austen could rely upon that tide of feeling to enlist support for the cause of Frederick Wentworth against the conceited selfishness of Sir Walter Elliot's social circle.

THE CHANGING NATURE OF SOCIETY

In the broader view, English society was undergoing dramatic, destabilising changes at the time Jane Austen was writing. Industrialisation, which had proceeded apace throughout the preceding half-century, was not only altering the appearance of the landscape, it was also modifying relationships between the social classes.

Although England was spared the turbulence of political revolution experienced in America and in France, the location of wealth and power within the population was changing. Throughout the eighteenth century, the middle classes had enjoyed great success in developing commercial activity. Technological improvements facilitated the spread of lucrative colonial activity abroad, while at home mechanical invention was transforming communications, labour patterns, and the supply of goods. Sir Walter Elliot's financial problems may in part be due to his own folly, but it seems equally likely that they are symptoms of economic pressures resultant from larger social change. The feudal relationships which had for centuries supported the lifestyle of the English aristocracy were rapidly being consigned to the past. Admiral Croft is able to afford the rent for Kellynch-hall as a consequence of his own enterprise and the exercise of his personal abilities.

Similarly, Sir Walter's snobbery is a personal weakness, but it may also reflect increased self-consciousness of class and social status in a society where their correlation to power could no longer be taken entirely for granted. Jane Austen wrote of what she knew, but close scrutiny of the apparently narrow field of her concerns can reveal a far broader depiction of changing England in the early nineteenth century.

LITERARY BACKGROUND

Jane Austen read extensively. Her father's library granted her access to a wide range of classical literature. Her taste in modern literature was formed through reading essayists such as Joseph Addison (1672–1719) and Sir Richard Steele (1672–1729), editors of *The Spectator*, and Dr Johnson (1709–84), whom she greatly admired. These writers sat in judgement upon contemporary social manners, and represented the sound common sense and respect for moderation that characterised the **Augustan** period.

Jane Austen read with admiration the novels of Samuel Richardson (1689–1761) and Henry Fielding (1707–1754), the most prominent of her predecessors in this relatively new genre. Although she found Henry Fielding excessively rumbustious on occasion, she recognised his great skill in contrivance of plot. She was particularly fond of Samuel Richardson's novel, *Sir Charles Grandison*, which she found commendable for the sustained roundedness of its characterisation. Her work fuses the strain of social **satire** in Fielding with the concerted anatomisation of love affairs in Richardson. From both writers she derived a sense that fiction could, like essays, offer moral guidance.

Women writers were also important to Jane Austen's development as a novelist. She read with admiration the novels of Fanny Burney (1752–1840), and with enjoyment the romantic fiction of Charlotte Smith (1749–1806). Amongst her contemporaries, she had particular regard for Maria Edgeworth (1767–1849). (From her own point of view, Maria Edgeworth wrote in a letter of the technical skill she found in *Persuasion*.) She was keenly aware of other women writing, but her sense of the restrictions on women publishing is reflected in Anne Elliot's impassioned discussion with Captain Harville. Harville cites literary evidence of women's fickleness. Anne replies by requesting:

> no reference to examples in books. Men have had every advantage of us in telling their own story. Education has been theirs in so much higher a degree; the pen has been in their hands. I will not allow books to prove any thing. (p. 237)

During the last decade of the eighteenth century the cultural movement known as **Romanticism** had taken hold in England. As Jane Austen was steeped in those values of common sense and moderation which made Dr Johnson such an important model for her, she initially responded by **satirising** the Romantic emphasis on the power of Nature and the priority of individual feelings.

She favoured sense over sensibility, and her early novels offer a corrective to the indulgence she perceived in a work such as Henry Mackenzie's *The Man of Feeling* (1771). *Northanger Abbey* is a notable **parody** of the conventions found in the **Gothic**, an emotive mode exemplified by the work of novelists such as Clara Reeve (1729–1807) and Ann Radcliffe (1764–1823).

The revolutionary politics and disruptive desires with which Romantic literature was associated were contrary to Jane Austen's view of the world, which valued stability and continuity. Nonetheless, the examination of personal feelings in relation to social etiquette that we encounter in *Persuasion* bears some of the hallmarks of the Romantic period. It is, after all, Lord Byron and Sir Walter Scott, not Samuel Johnson and Alexander Pope, who form the basis for Anne Elliot's literary discussion with Captain Benwick.

PART SIX

CRITICAL HISTORY AND BROADER PERSPECTIVES

CRITICAL RECEPTION

Sir Walter Scott is remembered primarily as a novelist today. Jane Austen read him with pleasure, and he was an appreciative reader of Jane Austen's fiction. A few years after her death, Sir Walter Scott wrote in a private journal of his admiration for the 'exquisite touch' with which her writing transformed a commonplace reality, in order to disclose its truth and so make it interesting. She exercised her great talent, he noted, without ostentation and without striving for effect.

Sir Walter Scott recognised peculiarly modern characteristics in Jane Austen's work, differentiating her from her eighteenth-century precursors. This view was later endorsed, in 1948, by the highly influential critic F.R. Leavis, who assigned Jane Austen an elevated status in *The Great Tradition*, as the fountainhead of the nineteenth-century novel. Leavis's endorsement consolidated a trend to regard Jane Austen as one of England's most significant writers. Lord Tennyson had ranked her second only to Shakespeare, back in 1860.

But overall there was surprisingly little interest in Jane Austen between her death in 1817, and 1870 when her nephew, Edward Austen-Leigh published *A Memoir of Jane Austen* (included in the Penguin Classics edition). *Persuasion* was largely ignored, although it was favourably reviewed by Archbishop Richard Whateley, in the *Quarterly Review* in 1821. He commended its easy amalgam of 'instruction and amusement', and argued that it was the finest of her novels. A collected edition of those novels appeared in 1833.

Following the *Memoir* interest grew steadily. Virginia Woolf, in *The Common Reader* (1925), regarded *Persuasion* as a technical advance on the earlier novels, showing a surer handling of the interior life of her heroine. She also remarked a harshness in the book's **satirical** tone. Virginia Woolf speculated that, had she lived, Jane Austen would have made more explicit inroads into the terrain later occupied by **psychological realism**. This would have made her the direct forerunner of Henry James, and Marcel Proust and, we should add, Virginia Woolf herself.

The assessments of *Persuasion* by Richard Whateley and Virginia Woolf, together with Sir Walter Scott's estimation, and the response of Jane Austen's contemporary Maria Edgeworth can be found, with other useful critical essays, in *Jane Austen: Northanger Abbey and Persuasion*, edited by B.C. Southam (London, 1976). F.R. Leavis's *The Great Tradition* is published by Penguin Books.

CONTEMPORARY APPROACHES

Late Victorian criticism tended to focus on character. Subsequent critics have shown more interest in formal and technical issues, as well as in the ethical problems raised by *Persuasion*. Increasingly, contemporary critics have attended to the political implications of Jane Austen's work. An important book in shifting the emphasis of critical attention was Marilyn Butler's *Jane Austen and the War of Ideas* (Oxford, 1975). The following three approaches give some indication of the sorts of issues now being considered.

FEMINIST

The term 'feminist criticism' covers a range of approaches crucially concerned with the representation of women, their personal identities, and their social relationships within a society dominated by men. It is not surprising that Jane Austen has received broad and varied feminist analysis.

Some critics have discovered a significant number of neglected women novelists, and have sought to re-evaluate Jane Austen in the light of this submerged tradition. Notable in this enterprise is Sandra M. Gilbert and Susan Gubar's *The Madwoman in the Attic: the Woman Writer and the Nineteenth-century Literary Imagination* (New Haven, 1979).

Other critics have explored particular thematic concerns of the fiction in order to disclose ways in which Jane Austen's view of the world was shaped in relation to her social status as a woman. For example, Julia Prewitt Brown, in *Jane Austen's Novels* (Cambridge, Mass., 1979) explores the contemporary cult of the family, and the value Jane Austen discovered in domesticity.

Other critics have read Jane Austen's fiction in the light of political positions taken by feminism during her lifetime, and subsequently. For example, Margaret Kirkham, *Jane Austen: Feminism and Fiction* (Brighton, 1983), and Mary Poovey, *The Proper Lady and the Woman Writer* (Chicago, 1984).

HISTORICIST

Historicist analysis takes many forms, but aims to locate the work in relation to the social context of its writing. It usually assembles information which enables the critic to trace the operation of historical forces through the text.

The society of which Jane Austen wrote was stratified, with clear class divisions. Her fiction draws almost exclusively upon the lives of the English gentry, and her horizons fall squarely within the Tory political landscape. A Marxist analysis would draw attention to the class divisions supporting her privileged stratum of society, raising the issue of those conditions endured by servants and by members of the working class. Industrial England was a reality which is significantly absent from her fiction.

A notable historicist study of Jane Austen is Warren Roberts's *Jane Austen and the French Revolution* (London, 1979). Also relevant, despite its lack of direct reference to *Persuasion*, is Nancy Armstrong's *Desires and Domestic Fiction: A Political History of the Novel* (Oxford, 1987).

POST-COLONIAL

The critic Edward Said has taken a prominent role in indicating how the fortunes of characters in European novels may conceal the exploitation of women and men in remote colonies. Amongst Jane Austen's novels, Said has paid particular attention to *Mansfield Park*, but it is possible to apply his approach to *Persuasion*, noting the references to the West Indies, especially as the source of Mrs Smith's improved circumstances. The material and human resources of those islands were the basis for much European wealth.

See, Edward Said, *Culture and Imperialism* (London, 1993).

World events		Jane Austen	Literature & arts
	1795	*Sense and Sensibility* completed	Maria Edgeworth, *Letters for Literary Ladies*
			Thomas Chatterton (d. 1770), *Poetical works*
Napoleon Bonaparte leads the French army and conquers most of Italy	**1796**	*Pride and Prejudice* completed	Fanny Burney, *Camilla, or a Picture of Youth*
			Samuel Taylor Coleridge, *Poems on Various Subjects*
British naval victories over the French at Cape St Vincent and over the Dutch at Camperdown	**1797**		Ann Radcliff, *The Italian*
Nelson defeats the French at the Battle of Aboukir Bay	**1798**	*Northanger Abbey* completed	William Wordsworth and Samuel Taylor Coleridge, *Lyrical Ballads*
			Maria Edgeworth, *Practical Education*
Coalition of Britain, Russia, Portugal, Naples and the Ottoman Empire against France	**1799**		Clara Reeve, *Destination*
Act of Union unites Great Britain and Ireland to form the United Kingdom	**1800**		William Wordsworth, in preface to second edition of *Lyrical Ballads*, defines poetic Romanticism
			Maria Edgeworth, *Castle Rackrent*

World events		Jane Austen	Literature & arts
British naval victory over the Danes at Copenhagen	**1801**	Austen family move to Bath	Maria Edgeworth, *Belinda*
Napoleon becomes President of the Italian Republic, and is made First Consul of France for life Peace Treaty of Amiens between Britain and France	**1802**		
War resumes between Britain and France because of disputes over Malta, Switzerland and Italy. Continues until 1815	**1803**		Lady Mary Montague (d. 1762), *Works, Including Letters*
Bonaparte is crowned Emperor of the French. Preparations along the English coast against possible French invasion	**1804**		Maria Edgeworth, *A Modern Griselda*
Battle of Trafalgar: Nelson defeats Franco-Spanish fleet, but is mortally wounded	**1805**	Death of Jane Austen's father, George Austen	William Wordsworth completes a major draft of *The Prelude*
Napoleon continues conquest of Europe	**1806**		Maria Edgeworth, *Leonora* Walter Scott, *Ballads and Lyrical Pieces*
The slave trade is abolished in British territories	**1807**		First published poetry collection by Lord Byron, *Hours of Idleness; Poems on Various Occasions*

World events		Jane Austen	Literature & arts
Start of British involvement in the Peninsular War	1808		Walter Scott, *Marmion; A Tale of Flodden Field*
British victory at Talavera in Spain	1809	Jane Austen and her mother and sister move to Chawton	Maria Edgeworth, *Tales of Fashionable Life*
Napoleon annexes Holland	1810		Walter Scott, *The Lady of the Lake*
	1811	*Sense and Sensibility* published	
Napoleon invades Russia; winter forces him to retreat and decimates his army	1812		Lord Byron, first two cantos of *Childe Harold's Pilgrimage*
Napoleon is defeated by the Allies at the battle of Leipzig Wellington drives the French from Spain	1813	*Pride and Prejudice* published	Percy Bysshe Shelley, *Queen Mab*
Wellington's victory at Battle of Toulouse ends Peninsular War Napoleon abdicates and is exiled to Elba	1814	*Mansfield Park* published	Walter Scott publishes *Waverley*, his first novel Fanny Burney, *The Wanderer* Maria Edgeworth, *Patronage*
Napoleon escapes from Elba and marches on Paris; within three weeks he is Emperor again, but is defeated by Wellington at Waterloo; he abdicates and is banished to St Helena Second Peace Treaty of Paris between Allies and France	1815	Begins writing **Persuasion**	Walter Scott, *Guy Mannering*

World events		Jane Austen	Literature & arts
	1816	*Emma* published **Persuasion** completed	Walter Scott, *The Antiquary* Samuel Taylor Coleridge, *Christabel and Other Poems;* includes 'Kubla Khan' and 'A Vision in a Dream' Benjamin Constant, *Adolphe*
	1817	Jane Austen moves to Winchester; dies in July	Walter Scott, *Rob Roy*
	1818	*Northanger Abbey* and *Persuasion* published posthumously	Walter Scott, *The Heart of Midlothian* Mary Wollstonecroft Shelley, *Frankenstein, or the Modern Prometheus* John Keats, *Endymion*
	1819		Walter Scott, *Ivanhoe*
George III dies; succeeded by George IV	**1820**		John Keats, *Lamia and Other Poems;* includes 'Eve of St Agnes' and his main odes ('Grecian Urn'; 'Nightingale'; 'Autumn') Percy Bysshe Shelley, *Prometheus Unbound;* also published: 'Ode to the West Wind' and 'To a Skylark' John Clare, *Poems, Descriptive of Rural Life*
Napoleon I dies on St Helena	**1821**		Walter Scott, *Kenilworth* Thomas de Quincey, *The Confessions of an English Opium-Eater*

ambiguity the capacity of words and sentences to have double, multiple, or uncertain meanings

ambivalence the coexistence of different feelings or attitudes towards the same object

anachronism the inclusion of an element in a literary work which is out of time with the historical period of the setting

Augustan a name applied to writing from the first half of the eighteenth century, that placed special emphasis upon moderation, good taste, and social decorousness

caricature an exaggeration of personality traits resulting in a rendering of character that is ridiculous or grotesque

chivalric romance primarily medieval fictions portraying the exploits of knights, highlighting their codes of conduct, including that which governed love and courtship

epistolary written in the form of letters

free indirect style a technique of narrating the thoughts, decisions, and speech of a character through a particular amalgam of first-person and third-person narrative

Gothic fictional mode concentrating on the bizarre and macabre, or on aberrant psychological states. There was a pronounced flourishing of Gothic fictions at the end of the eighteenth century

irony basically, a mode of expression in which one thing is said while another is meant. Irony can also occur in narrative situations, where either the reader is aware of meaning which is not apparent to the characters, or the situation has particular significance for one of the characters but not for the others

melodrama writing that relies upon sensational happenings, violent action, and improbable events

metaphor description of one thing as being another thing

parody an imitation of a specific work of literature, or of a style, devised so as to ridicule its characteristic features

pathetic fallacy term, first applied by John Ruskin in 1856, identifying the habit of certain writers to equate their own or their character's mood with aspects of the world around them, such as the weather

psychological realism a mode of fiction which renders the inner lives of characters, rather than concentrating on external actions

Romantic referring to a phase in English literature between 1789 and 1830, characterised by a heightened emphasis upon human feelings and the vital force of nature. Note that 'romantic' is a quite distinct adjective, applied to amorous adventures, and affairs of the heart, without reference to a specific period

satire writing that exposes and ridicules human foibles

sensibility indicating a refined capacity to feel. A literature of sensibility, which tended to portray heightened emotional states, in an often overwrought manner, became popular in the latter part of the eighteenth century

stream of consciousness a narrative technique allowing access to the multifarious contents of the mind of a character or characters. Dorothy Richardson and Virginia Woolf were notable exponents of this technique

AUTHOR OF THIS NOTE

Dr Julian Cowley taught English at King's College London before joining the University of Luton, where he is Senior Lecturer in Literary Studies.

Notes

NOTES

Notes

Notes

NOTES

York Notes Advanced

Margaret Atwood
The Handmaid's Tale

Jane Austen
Mansfield Park

Jane Austen
Persuasion

Jane Austen
Pride and Prejudice

Alan Bennett
Talking Heads

William Blake
*Songs of Innocence and of
Experience*

Charlotte Brontë
Jane Eyre

Emily Brontë
Wuthering Heights

Geoffrey Chaucer
The Franklin's Tale

Geoffrey Chaucer
*General Prologue to the
Canterbury Tales*

Geoffrey Chaucer
*The Wife of Bath's Prologue
and Tale*

Joseph Conrad
Heart of Darkness

Charles Dickens
Great Expectations

John Donne
Selected Poems

George Eliot
The Mill on the Floss

F. Scott Fitzgerald
The Great Gatsby

E.M. Forster
A Passage to India

Brian Friel
Translations

Thomas Hardy
The Mayor of Casterbridge

Thomas Hardy
Tess of the d'Urbervilles

Seamus Heaney
*Selected Poems from Opened
Ground*

Nathaniel Hawthorne
The Scarlet Letter

James Joyce
Dubliners

John Keats
Selected Poems

Christopher Marlowe
Doctor Faustus

Arthur Miller
Death of a Salesman

Toni Morrison
Beloved

William Shakespeare
Antony and Cleopatra

William Shakespeare
As You Like It

William Shakespeare
Hamlet

William Shakespeare
King Lear

William Shakespeare
Measure for Measure

William Shakespeare
The Merchant of Venice

William Shakespeare
Much Ado About Nothing

William Shakespeare
Othello

William Shakespeare
Romeo and Juliet

William Shakespeare
The Tempest

William Shakespeare
The Winter's Tale

Mary Shelley
Frankenstein

Alice Walker
The Color Purple

Oscar Wilde
*The Importance of Being
Earnest*

Tennessee Williams
A Streetcar Named Desire

John Webster
The Duchess of Malfi

W.B. Yeats
Selected Poems

OTHER TITLES

GCSE and equivalent levels

Maya Angelou
I Know Why the Caged Bird Sings

Jane Austen
Pride and Prejudice

Alan Ayckbourn
Absent Friends

Elizabeth Barrett Browning
Selected Poems

Robert Bolt
A Man for All Seasons

Harold Brighouse
Hobson's Choice

Charlotte Brontë
Jane Eyre

Emily Brontë
Wuthering Heights

Shelagh Delaney
A Taste of Honey

Charles Dickens
David Copperfield

Charles Dickens
Great Expectations

Charles Dickens
Hard Times

Charles Dickens
Oliver Twist

Roddy Doyle
Paddy Clarke Ha Ha Ha

George Eliot
Silas Marner

George Eliot
The Mill on the Floss

William Golding
Lord of the Flies

Oliver Goldsmith
She Stoops To Conquer

Willis Hall
The Long and the Short and the Tall

Thomas Hardy
Far from the Madding Crowd

Thomas Hardy
The Mayor of Casterbridge

Thomas Hardy
Tess of the d'Urbervilles

Thomas Hardy
The Withered Arm and other Wessex Tales

L.P. Hartley
The Go-Between

Seamus Heaney
Selected Poems

Susan Hill
I'm the King of the Castle

Barry Hines
A Kestrel for a Knave

Louise Lawrence
Children of the Dust

Harper Lee
To Kill a Mockingbird

Laurie Lee
Cider with Rosie

Arthur Miller
The Crucible

Arthur Miller
A View from the Bridge

Robert O'Brien
Z for Zachariah

Frank O'Connor
My Oedipus Complex and other stories

George Orwell
Animal Farm

J.B. Priestley
An Inspector Calls

Willy Russell
Educating Rita

Willy Russell
Our Day Out

J.D. Salinger
The Catcher in the Rye

William Shakespeare
Henry IV Part 1

William Shakespeare
Henry V

William Shakespeare
Julius Caesar

William Shakespeare
Macbeth

William Shakespeare
The Merchant of Venice

William Shakespeare
A Midsummer Night's Dream

William Shakespeare
Much Ado About Nothing

William Shakespeare
Romeo and Juliet

William Shakespeare
The Tempest

William Shakespeare
Twelfth Night

George Bernard Shaw
Pygmalion

Mary Shelley
Frankenstein

R.C. Sherriff
Journey's End

Rukshana Smith
Salt on the snow

John Steinbeck
Of Mice and Men

Robert Louis Stevenson
Dr Jekyll and Mr Hyde

Jonathan Swift
Gulliver's Travels

Robert Swindells
Daz 4 Zoe

Mildred D. Taylor
Roll of Thunder, Hear My Cry

Mark Twain
Huckleberry Finn

James Watson
Talking in Whispers

William Wordsworth
Selected Poems

A Choice of Poets

Mystery Stories of the Nineteenth Century including The Signalman

Nineteenth Century Short Stories

Poetry of the First World War

Six Women Poets

Chinua Achebe
Things Fall Apart

Edward Albee
Who's Afraid of Virginia Woolf?

Margaret Atwood
Cat's Eye

Jane Austen
Emma

Jane Austen
Northanger Abbey

Jane Austen
Sense and Sensibility

Samuel Beckett
Waiting for Godot

Robert Browning
Selected Poems

Robert Burns
Selected Poems

Angela Carter
Nights at the Circus

Geoffrey Chaucer
The Merchant's Tale

Geoffrey Chaucer
The Miller's Tale

Geoffrey Chaucer
The Nun's Priest's Tale

Samuel Taylor Coleridge
Selected Poems

Daniel Defoe
Moll Flanders

Daniel Defoe
Robinson Crusoe

Charles Dickens
Bleak House

Charles Dickens
Hard Times

Emily Dickinson
Selected Poems

Carol Ann Duffy
Selected Poems

George Eliot
Middlemarch

T.S. Eliot
The Waste Land

T.S. Eliot
Selected Poems

Henry Fielding
Joseph Andrews

E.M. Forster
Howards End

John Fowles
The French Lieutenant's Woman

Robert Frost
Selected Poems

Elizabeth Gaskell
North and South

Stella Gibbons
Cold Comfort Farm

Graham Greene
Brighton Rock

Thomas Hardy
Jude the Obscure

Thomas Hardy
Selected Poems

Joseph Heller
Catch-22

Homer
The Iliad

Homer
The Odyssey

Gerard Manley Hopkins
Selected Poems

Aldous Huxley
Brave New World

Kazuo Ishiguro
The Remains of the Day

Ben Jonson
The Alchemist

Ben Jonson
Volpone

James Joyce
A Portrait of the Artist as a Young Man

Philip Larkin
Selected Poems

D.H. Lawrence
The Rainbow

D.H. Lawrence
Selected Stories

D.H. Lawrence
Sons and Lovers

D.H. Lawrence
Women in Love

John Milton
Paradise Lost Bks I & II

John Milton
Paradise Lost Bks IV & IX

Thomas More
Utopia

Sean O'Casey
Juno and the Paycock

George Orwell
Nineteen Eighty-four

John Osborne
Look Back in Anger

Wilfred Owen
Selected Poems

Sylvia Plath
Selected Poems

Alexander Pope
Rape of the Lock and other poems

Ruth Prawer Jhabvala
Heat and Dust

Jean Rhys
Wide Sargasso Sea

William Shakespeare
As You Like It

William Shakespeare
Coriolanus

William Shakespeare
Henry IV Pt 1

William Shakespeare
Henry V

William Shakespeare
Julius Caesar

William Shakespeare
Macbeth

William Shakespeare
Measure for Measure

William Shakespeare
A Midsummer Night's Dream

William Shakespeare
Richard II

William Shakespeare
Richard III

William Shakespeare
Sonnets

William Shakespeare
The Taming of the Shrew

William Shakespeare
Twelfth Night

William Shakespeare
The Winter's Tale

George Bernard Shaw
Arms and the Man

George Bernard Shaw
Saint Joan

Muriel Spark
The Prime of Miss Jean Brodie

John Steinbeck
The Grapes of Wrath

John Steinbeck
The Pearl

Tom Stoppard
Arcadia

Tom Stoppard
*Rosencrantz and Guildenstern
are Dead*

Jonathan Swift
*Gulliver's Travels and The
Modest Proposal*

Alfred, Lord Tennyson
Selected Poems

W.M. Thackeray
Vanity Fair

Virgil
The Aeneid

Edith Wharton
The Age of Innocence

Tennessee Williams
Cat on a Hot Tin Roof

Tennessee Williams
The Glass Menagerie

Virginia Woolf
Mrs Dalloway

Virginia Woolf
To the Lighthouse

William Wordsworth
Selected Poems

Metaphysical Poets